For Neil, Emily & Melissa.

D.

# Contents

# Foreword

Well, who'd be a freelance journalist these days? There are far easier ways to earn a living. Publications are closing, rates are being squeezed, and surveys show that journalists rate just below traffic wardens and tax inspectors in popularity.

And yet it's not all bad – the huge explosion in online publishing has meant that there are now more outlets for your writing than ever before. And a writer can find themselves doing jobs that didn't even exist ten years ago, such as running a blog for a client, or getting hired to tweet.

In the last year alone, I've had overseas trips, rubbed shoulders with celebrities and made it into publications read by millions. But more importantly for me, I have the flexibility to work around my family, work from home and the choice to take the afternoon off if I want. I have a career that I'm in charge of, doing what I love.

But it's not all about the perks – I think that writing is something that you're called to do. When I am coaching journalists, even though they express frustrations about the business, the bottom line is – they can never imagine doing anything else. They don't want to do anything else, even though other careers might seem easier.

And if being a writer is your calling, I can tell you for definite that that calling never goes away – it just gets louder. Don't try to ignore your urge to write because it's not going anywhere.

So, if you have a call to write, to turn that into a skill you can make a living from, you're going to need some help. Whether you're already working as a freelance or taking your writing from a hobby to a profession, you'll learn a lot from these pages.

I think that the biggest mistake we can make as writers is to assume that we know all about what we're doing. There is always more to learn – new methods of marketing, new avenues to explore, new people to talk to who will inspire fresh ideas.

The great thing about this book's author, Linda Jones, is that not only does she have the wisdom of what it takes to do this job well, she's willing to share it.

Good luck and happy writing!

All the best

Joanne Mallon

*Joanne Mallon is a freelance writer, she also coaches journalists and editors to help them get better at what they do. www.MediaLifeCoach.com www.JoannetheCoach.com*

# Introduction

There is no doubt that times are tougher than ever for many freelance writers. Many long established publications have now folded or had their freelance budgets removed.

Online, there's no end of opportunities to write but few are well paid or even paid at all. Why would anyone bother to become a freelance writer in such dire circumstances? Lots of experienced freelancers may say 'don't bother' – and some are quitting to find more stable means of employment. Nobody could blame them.

I'd also say 'don't bother – don't bother, that is, unless you are prepared to work hard, to market yourself and set yourself apart from the competition, learning new skills along the way.' If you are good at what you do, meet deadlines, supply excellent copy and build strong relationships with your editors, then you still have a chance.

You need an endless supply of timely ideas, an old fashioned nose for a story and a strong work ethic. You also need to be ready to adapt and continue to learn, be inspired by innovative writers and editors, fully exploring the potential of newer media practises and new ways of investigating, reporting and reading.

This book does not give you a magic wand to wave to transform your life into an never-ending round of exciting commissions, work coming out of your ears and a client list to die for. Instead, it offers down to earth, straight-talking advice to allow you to make your own way in this most competitive of fields – and understand what you are up against. This comes from my own experience and some of the advice included comes from hard lessons learned.

I've been a freelance writer since 1998, and, in 2003, I set up the agency Passionate Media, we now specialise in all sorts of words – from journalism to social media and a smidgen of media relations thrown in too (I never thought I'd see the day). The tips in this book come from what has worked for me, they have helped people on training workshops I run, colleagues at Passionate Media and writers I have mentored. I hope they work for you too.

There's a definite bias in favour of journalistic writing, with more commercially-minded endeavours also included in these pages. This is where my experience lies.

Writing is a tough old business – and I love it. I've built a company out of my freelance writing career and consider myself very lucky and privileged to make a living out of something that I enjoy so much.

But that's not to say it has been easy. Anyone who goes into freelancing thinking the streets are paved with gold needs to get a grip. Make sure you are going in with your eyes wide open.

The best way to get ahead in freelancing is possibly to start by looking for a part-time job. Yes really. It is very unlikely (but not impossible) that you can make a good living straight away with no experience in publishing or the media. You need to build up contacts and establish a reputation. Unfortunately, neither of these pays the bills.

This book is designed for those at the start of a freelance writing career, but might also be of help to those who have already made some progress.

My aim was to offer realistic advice. It's not a complete, step-by-step guide to freelancing success. Nor is it a 'How to write' guide. I'm clinging on to a belief that anyone wanting to make a living from writing might already have an inkling of how to do that.

Good luck.

# CHAPTER ONE

# Freelance Writing

**Freelance Writing**

Published by:
Greatest Guides Limited, Woodstock, Bridge End, Warwick CV34 6PD, United Kingdom

www.greatestguides.com

Every effort has been made to ensure that this book contains accurate and current information. However, neither the author nor the publisher shall be liable for any loss or damage suffered by readers as a result of any information contained herein.

All trademarks are acknowledged as belonging to their respective companies.

**Author Acknowledgments**

Thanks to everyone I have interviewed for this book, to the members at the JournoBiz forum who have been a source of support since 2003 and to Joanne Mallon for her contribution and foreword. Thanks to Nick Daws for his input. Many thanks to all the bloggers who have taught me so much over the years, to Craig McGinty for his wisdom and to my colleagues at Passionate Media for all their help.

Greatest Guides is committed to a sustainable future for our planet. This book is printed on paper certified by the Forest Stewardship Council.

MIX
Paper
FSC FSC® C020837

Printed and bound in the United Kingdom

LLYFRGELLOEDD POWYS LIBRARIES

ISBN 978-1-907906-20-6

# Getting
# Started

*" The role of a writer is not to say what we all can say, but what we are unable to say. "*

Anaïs Nin

# Chapter 1
# Getting Started

## SIX OF THE BEST: MYTHS ABOUT FREELANCE WRITING

1.  **It will make you rich – and quickly**

    Excuse me while I stop laughing. You're not going to get paid on time, every time. Get used to this prospect but determine to do all you can to stop it happening.

2.  **Writing an article in full before sending it to an editor is always a good idea**

    No. This isn't right. The pitch is the thing.

3.  **Editors are all ogres**

    They're not.

4.  **Your writing talent is the single, most important factor in your success**

    It isn't. The ability to find stuff to write about, to elicit the right information and to chase for payment, should all be jostling for position at the top of that list.

5.  **It has to be an isolated pursuit**

    Oh no. You can embrace all sorts of opportunities online to make new contacts and friends as well as real life networking opportunities. Don't think you have to be lonely.

6.  **It's easy**

It's not. If that were the case, everyone would be doing it. Plenty try and fail. Give yourself the best shot by learning all you can to do it properly.

## FIRST THINGS FIRST

### Writing as a business

Remember at all times that, if you are serious about making a living from freelance writing, then you have to take it seriously. You think I'm stating the obvious, don't you? I'm not, I promise; I have encountered too many wannabe writers over the years who reckon they can rake in the riches by sending out articles and hoping for the best. If you are going to work for yourself, then guess what, you're setting up a business. Get all the advice you can on that, and, if it all sounds a bit scary, then it's not for you!

### Weigh up your business skills. Is self-employment going to be for you?

Have you heard that 'turnover is vanity and profit is sanity?' or that 'thinking outside the box can lead to joined up thinking?' You probably have and you may have rolled your eyes at such gobbledegook.

It may sound like a load of old nonsense to you, as a clever and motivated 'creative type' – and nobody really has to talk like that.

But the first of these hackneyed expressions is actually spot on. Keeping costs down is one of the most important areas of business, especially when starting out.

### *Also important here:* Don't try and be someone you're not

There are people who will have different ideas about what is 'professional' and what isn't.

For some in business, the prevailing view is that you have to talk in riddles and dress to kill. But that's simply not the case. You can do well if you relax, be confident and be yourself.

Don't assume (like I did) that other people you meet in business know it all just because they have been running a business longer. They may not have the sort of attention to detail, people skills or work ethic that you have.

## SIX OF THE BEST: CHARACTERISTICS OF A FREELANCE WRITER

1. **Strong work ethic**

   Forget the fantasy of swanning around in your dressing gown, penning your oeuvre when the muse takes you. Right here's where you start paying – in sweat! (And okay, possibly in your dressing gown).

2. **In-built bullshit detector**

   Don't go anywhere without it. Question, question and question again.

3. **Tenacity**

   Try hard, then try harder. Never give up.

4. **Courage**

   A media career favours the brave.

5. **Willingness to push yourself forward, and/or market yourself**

   You can't hide your light under a bushel – shout from the rooftops about your experience and skill.

6. **…Writing talent**

   Yes it does matter – but possibly not as much as you think!

## WRITING AS A HOBBY

I wish you good luck with your hobby. Enjoy it, nurture it, take pride in it, notch up every success by shouting your achievement from the rooftops, but please don't make the mistake of thinking everyone will take you seriously. Beware of the editors you might find "ferocious". Research your target markets well (more on this later) and be prepared for a rocky road.

You may encounter writers who feel your willingness to do what they do for a living for fun undermines their professional skills and devalues them. You may not agree but it's a commonly held view among established freelancers.

## REALITY CHECK: MANAGE YOUR EXPECTATIONS

Think about what you are expecting from your writing endeavours – if you are anticipating editors calling you, offering exciting assignments for pots of money within weeks of starting out, then you need to come down off your cloud and decide how you can really make a go of things. Set targets for what you would like to achieve month by month, whether that's alongside your current full-time or part-time job, or to make your hobby profitable, and do all you can to reach those realistic goals.

## ASK YOURSELF:

What sort of work can I be confident of finding?

Think you are going to be jetting off to film premiere to interview the stars, or test-driving the latest Mercedes because you fancy giving it a go? Sounds good to me. But seriously, why would anyone in charge of such top jobs give them to anyone without proven experience? The reality of freelancing as a career, for many, is a constant whirl of mundane jobs, chasing payment and seeking new opportunities. So why do they do it? Well, in my case anyway, when these opportunities come off, it can be fantastic. I'm an optimist – you can make it as a freelance, but I'm a realist too.

## ASK YOURSELF:

And why will YOU make it, exactly?

For me, this is the key question. What can you offer editors that the millions of other aspiring or successful writers haven't tried already? Be honest with yourself. If you can't answer this question, then it might be time to move on and find something different. Writing for fun is one thing, but if all you are going to do is end up floundering because your ideas are the same as everyone else's, what's the point in clinging on to false hope?

I don't think I'm being unduly harsh here. Even the most established freelancers, with decades of experience in the media behind them, have so-called dry spells – otherwise known as the 'feast and famine' of freelance life. Take a long hard look at your experience, knowledge and skills, and don't kid yourself about how much you're going to starve!

## REALITY CHECK: WHO ARE YOU UP AGAINST?

In the long run, as you prove yourself, editors may sometimes come to you and ask you to do some work for them, as will commercial clients. But this won't happen until you have a reputation as someone who can deliver. And even then you are up against many, many other writers who have been around for years, delivering their perfectly clean, legally-sound, must-read copy to deadline.

## ORGANISATION, ORGANISATION, ORGANISATION

We've all heard the clichés about us "creative types" being a nightmare when it comes to paperwork, filing, and other admin stuff, haven't we? Well wouldn't you agree that these things often become clichés because they are rooted in truth? I am the world's worst record keeper (believe me, it's true) but these days I find myself surrounded by spreadsheets, job sheets, contact lists and update charts. How sad is that? But seriously, you have to find a way of keeping track of your efforts, including work done, pitches sent, money owing, and ideas for future projects. I've included some examples of paperwork that could be useful in chapter 10.

## TIME IS OF THE ESSENCE

When are you going to write? Think you can just fit it in with all the rest of the demands of your busy day? Who's going to do all the other stuff you have to do, if you lock yourself away in your back bedroom with nothing but your computer for company? It's vital to plan your time. Are you a morning or evening person? Can you burn the midnight oil? Do you really have to watch the latest instalment of your favourite quiz show, soap or sports update when you could be knocking out 500 words instead? Be ruthless, declutter your day.

## WORKING FOR YOURSELF

Are you unemployable? I know I am. I have already listed some key attributes of freelance writers, but, before you take the leap, here are some other factors that could determine your success:

You:

- Couldn't work for anyone else

- Have the support of those around you

- Come from a family of people who have set up their own businesses and have seen the demands of self-employment at first hand

## BUSINESS PLAN BASICS

Write down your:

- Incomings and outgoings.

- Targets: How much do you need to earn, how are you going to do this?

- Budgets: What savings or capital, if any, do you have to invest in training and marketing activity?

- Projections: Where will you aim to be in six months to a year or more and how will you get there?

- Timescales for achieving these.

## PLAN YOUR MARKETING

Include:

Who will buy your work.

How you're going to reach them and when.

Where you will work. Focus on every detail of how you believe your freelance writing business will work.

## WORKING FROM HOME

Ask yourself:

Am I being realistic?

Can I earn enough for this to be my sole income?

Can I organise my work well enough?

Can I burn the midnight oil to earn enough?

Am I self-motivated enough or will the lure of daytime TV be too strong?

Will I feel lonely?

## SOME POINTS TO REMEMBER IF YOU HAVE YOUNG CHILDREN:

Don't expect to be able to work while they sleep or play around you.

This especially applies to making phone calls – I have learned from bitter experience.

Make child care arrangements just as if you were going out to work.

Organise your day so that you get quality time with your family – not sitting at your computer when you could be reading a bedtime story, if you would really rather be doing that.

Consider finding a shared office space with other writers. If you have to conduct interviews, then where can you do this? Expecting your contacts to step over Barbies with no heads on or Buzz Lightyear toys might be a bit much!

## GET TO GRIPS WITH GRAMMAR

"Don't worry about spelling, just tell the story!" Every time I hear of someone dishing out this advice, I want to bang my head on the table.

It might be sound guidance if you are in a room with other would-be storytellers, working on a joint project for fun, but if you ever present an editor with a piece of work where the apostrophes are nowhere to be seen, or you have written 'there' for 'their' (I've seen worse), then you can bank on not being very well thought of to the point you may not be called on to write for them again. Make Lynn Truss the best mate you ever had. If, at this point, you're asking "Who?" then you may want to look it up.

## GET TO GRIPS WITH COPYRIGHT

Aspiring and new writers can appear to find the issue of copyright rather vexing. It doesn't have to be. In a lot of people's minds, it really is quite simple.

You will retain copyright of your work unless you sell the licence to reproduce it to a publisher outright, so a copyright sign isn't needed.

Placing the copyright symbol, with your name and the date/year of when something was written, is usually sufficient to protect your material.

If you want extra peace of mind that your work is safe from being copied, you can undertake some additional measures. You may add a legal phrase at the bottom of a page (print or web) saying something like "This work is the property of the author and may not be used or reproduced under any circumstances." There are many examples of so-called copyright terms on the web. You may alter the wording to suit your preference. You can find other phrases in use if you look at various websites or other resources (see Recommended Reading if you are looking for inspiration).

But, and it's a big but, I really wouldn't go down the "extra protection" route. If you have an exclusive interview with Madonna on the adoption of a child, or a piece shedding light on an explosive political scandal, then maybe this is justified. But, as a beginner, I'd say you're more likely to annoy the people you're writing for than impress them.

## GET TO GRIPS WITH LIBEL AND CONTEMPT

There's not an editor in the land who will knowlingly publish your work if it contains a legal howler. Get yourself a copy of the most recent McNae's Essential Law for Journalists and make sure you understand what on earth it's talking about. Some might protest that it's not needed in today's ever-changing writing world. Well they're wrong.

Newspaper and magazines can call on their legal teams to check whether anything that is deliberately provocative is "safe", but, as a writer, you don't have that luxury. Don't ruin your reputation as a "safe pair of hands" before you've even got off the ground. Find out about media law and stay well within it.

Perhaps you may consider that you will be writing about totally non-controversial topics and this advice is superfluous. But it doesn't matter whether you are writing about home interiors, TV, knitting, political scandals or mass murder, it's still imperative that you learn about these laws and what they cover.

## IN THE DARK ABOUT PITCHES?

Some people still believe that the way to an editor's heart is to send them a complete article. There may be exceptions that prove the rule but, in general, what you must do is send your chosen editor a carefully crafted proposal of what you would like to write about. This proposal is called a pitch. In the US, you may see it referred to as a query.

Sending in the full article is known as writing on spec. There are times when writing 'on spec' might be called for, but please, as you start on a path to freelance writing, don't be under any misapprehension that this is in any way the norm. Editors want to see ideas, or 'pitches', and these need to be as tightly and professionally presented as possible. More on this in chapter four.

## ASK YOURSELF: CAN I TRUST THIS ADVICE?

Every aspiring writer knows there's a world of resources to tap into, to help chase their elusive dream of hitting the big time, but beware, please don't jump head first into buying a course off the Internet or believing everything you read. Take all promises of freelance wealth with a pinch of salt. There are freelance writers who earn six-figure sums, but, for every one of these, there are ten struggling hacks waiting to find out where their next commission will be coming from.

Find out all you can about any tutor or training site first. Who are they? What have they written? How often have they been published? Where can you read their work, and why are they tutoring? Ask them for testimonials from former pupils willing to put their full name to fulsome praise about their inspiration. I once shelled out for an online course about 'Writing for the Internet'. When I saw how much of it was about writing for free, I asked for my money back.

## AIM HIGH, START LOW

Never miss an opportunity when you're starting out, even if the pay isn't great and the work isn't something you'd want to do forever. You never know what something might lead to or how much work might come out of it. Cuttings of published work will be like gold dust to you in the early days. But, having said that, be wary of all 'writing for free' opportunities. See Chapter three for more on this.

When you're starting out as a freelance journalist, how realistic is it to write for mass circulation publications? It's not that easy. Yes, some people get lucky and enjoy instant success, and good luck to them, but a one-off piece placed does not make a whole career.

In my opinion, it all comes down to knowing you can deliver. If you aren't sure, you shouldn't pitch.

Having encouraged work experience people, students, trainees and wannabe freelance journalists over the years, what strikes me isn't their lack of writing skills. I'm sure they can write better than I can in lots of cases.

But what can irk me is an apparent lack of grasp on reality. You can't just pick a subject, say you are going to write about it, and expect an editor to commission you. And if they do – are you sure you know what to do?

## SUBMITTING A FEATURE NEEDS MORE THAN WRITING SKILLS

Can you expect the people you are going to write about to be found easily? Will they agree to speak to you?

You may have to ask difficult questions, and make sure all relevant details are included – all in a given word count. If your editor checks on certain questions you need to have asked of your interviewees, then it may be tempting to respond: "Oh, they didn't say." The point is that you should have asked. Put yourself in your readers' shoes – what will they want to know from your feature?

Personally, I wouldn't encourage being over ambitious – but there will always be exceptions, if the idea or story is good enough then it's going to get in.

There are also slots that can be filled by anyone who can write, and there have been some excellent success stories from students and 'newbie' writers. But you should make sure you learn the basics first.

That said, recognise your strengths – especially if you have spent time as a staff journalist in the regions or in another related position.

## BUILD YOUR CONFIDENCE – ESPECIALLY IF YOU HAVE ALREADY WORKED AS A STAFF WRITER

Worried you may not cut the mustard or that the commissioning editors could eat you alive? There's no need. If you've produced enough praiseworthy copy to satisfy the daily or weekly demands of a busy local news desk, then forget any qualms about making the jump. And if you are completely new to writing, give yourself the best shot by making sure your pitch is as good as it can be.

My own experience proves that confidence may not always be at a premium, if you decide to move on from a regional paper. Your stories may have been thrown back at you a million times or the air turned blue when you spectacularly failed to pull off a supposedly straightforward door-knock.

The temptation is to think that news or features editors on the nationals, for whom you hope to work in a freelance career, are bound to be even more ferocious – isn't it in the job description? Not necessarily.

Since I went freelance 11 years ago, such fears have proved ungrounded for me.

For freelance Guardian columnist, Michael Cross, the thought that anyone working on a regional paper wouldn't be seen as a "good bet" for working on a national is "horrifying". Adherence to media law, deadlines, and even the dreaded shorthand, should provide a solid grounding, he says.

"One of the best things about working on a local paper is how close you can get to the readers and their point of view.

"Not just when they ring you but when you see them day in, day out. When you lose sight of your readers then it can be dangerous," Michael continues.

## ADVICE FOR REGIONAL JOURNALISTS GOING FREELANCE

I've learned some hard lessons. Although I left regional papers under different circumstances to redundancy (I needed to go away and be a mum), these pointers are based on the sorts of experiences anyone moving on from local papers to work for themselves are bound to encounter. In these toughest of times, I'd say they are more important than ever.

## BE THANKFUL FOR YOUR TRANSFERABLE SKILLS

You know you can write, you know you can get on with people, you know you can work quickly and well under pressure and that you can meet strict deadlines.

For some, that may be despite what people around you have told you for however long you have slogged away in your current or last job.

But did you know that this makes you a prime candidate for a wide range of projects? Work is still out there for you to find. Value the strengths a career in regional news has given you and think about how to make the best of them, as well as convincing other people they're worth paying for.

What sort of work do I mean? Anywhere the gift of the gab (that's communications skills for my friends in PR), an approachable manner and a knowledge of how the media works are key skills needed. Did I say 'key skills?' isn't that the sort of corporate nonsense you can spot at a hundred paces? Yes it is. And there are people who will pay you good money to turn it into plain English.

## FORGET ANY "THEM AND US" NOTION YOU HAVE ABOUT NATIONALS AND THE REGIONALS

Learn how to pitch national news and features editors as effectively as possible.

Yes, markets are shrinking and budgets are being cut, but a cracking tale, sent to the right desk at the right time, will still sell. It just has to be better than it ever was and stand out more.

Don't worry about the reception you will get as a 'newbie' to this pitching lark.

If you can write a regional splash on deadline, you can sure as hell master 1,000 words with a couple of case studies and some expert comment in the time you're given to turn it around for a broadsheet section or monthly magazine.

And if you have a great 'human interest' story, study the tabloids and women's weeklies to see if you can flog an exclusive.

The features desks can be really quite nice when you ring them up, so long as you pick your moment well and convince them you can deliver.

It's funny; the better your story, the nicer they are.

Also, don't take rejection personally.

Business advisers have told me 'no can often mean not yet.'

So, that piece you suggested to an editor last week that was knocked back, or ignored, can still be sold elsewhere. Or it could be adapted for future use or even successfully slipped back under the nose of the same editor in the future.

## LOOK AFTER YOUR CONTACTS AND TAKE THEM WITH YOU

People you've already met as a reporter can still supply you with stories for a long time to come – but you can be more ambitious about where those stories will end up.

## CONSIDER MEDIA RELATIONS

It's not for everyone and it may not be for you. For many, it's a crying shame that that's where the work is.

Yet others will question how "objective" the media group you were working for was anyway.

Is churning out copy from other people's press releases really so 'morally superior' to doing PR for a charity you believe in? How can you ever join the ranks of the people you have taken such joy from insulting all these years?

Can you really afford to write it off completely?

So many questions!

But working in PR can also be fun. Think about what PR, if any, you could get fired up about doing and how you could square this with other work.

Be clear about where the edges of journalism and PR may blur in a client's mind and think carefully about avoiding conflicts of interest and not impinging on freelance news reporting or feature writing work.

Transparency is paramount.

## INVEST IN TRAINING

The NUJ, **www.journalism.co.uk** and other respected organisations run some brilliant courses. From business skills for journalists to how to do 'real life features'. There's a lot of help out there – and some of it will suit you and needn't cost the earth.

## NETWORK, NETWORK, NETWORK

I don't mean spend *all* your time at the local business breakfast networking club, asking the local undertaker if he needs someone to write a flyer to put through people's doors.

But it would be a good idea to at least find out about these sorts of organisations and if they are for you. They can and do bring in business and writers can be very active members – but it all depends on the chemistry and personality of the people in the group – most of all you.

But that's not all there is to networking. Get yourself in front of people you hope to work for and build relationships. That can be face to face, by email or online.

## GET TO GRIPS WITH SOCIAL NETWORKING

Twitter and facebook are your friends. Consider setting up your own blog. There's no end of pieces to be found online explaining how journalists can get the best out of them. Also, if you haven't yet caught the blogging bug, at least consider it. Lots of people will tell you it's a waste of time. Others, like Craig McGinty, a former Lancashire newspaper journalist, or Edinburgh-based Amber McNaught will tell you it can earn enough to do it full-time.

I've included lots more advice on this in chapter eight.

## DON'T COMPETE ON PRICE

If you haven't worked for yourself before, this may sound a bit of an alien concept. It certainly did for me in the early days of my writing business. But it's a very important factor in progressing, so getting to grips with it early on will bring you benefits.

It's tempting, when you start out working for yourself, to tell potential clients (whether it's an editor, a possible commercial writing client or someone who wants a script written for a public sector DVD) that you are cheap and you can beat what the next writer will do the job for.

Please don't do that. If you compete on price, you will lose the job on price. Your customer will move on to the next supplier when they come along with an even lower fee. As someone who now commissions work from others, in the words of Shania Twain, that don't impress me much. I'm talking from bitter experience.

What should you do instead? Work hard to convince them you are the best for the job, because you'll do the best job. Be prepared to explain why your commercial writing services are worth paying more for. What can you do that others can't? What can you guarantee? (This can be something as simple as a promise you will always reply to messages within 24 hours and/or that you will provide detailed work breakdowns or treat clients with professionalism at all times).

You want people to want to be able to afford you because you are the best for the job.

If they want you enough, and have the money, they'll find a way.

Do you really want to work for them if they have no money and don't really want you?

## OTHER IMPORTANT MONEY MATTERS:

* Avoid dropping your price or offering to do something for free, if you can help it, thinking this will get your foot in the door. It often doesn't. Many people do it and so have I, but, in the long run, experience has shown that it can bring huge disappointment.

* Don't take any work on, even from people you trust, are friends with, have worked with before, or are existing contacts, without them signing all paperwork up front. Put paperwork in place to make that happen (More in chapter 10).

* Master all aspects of contracts, order forms and terms and conditions. If you can, ask customers to pay up front, either the whole fee or some of it. Their reaction *may* give you a big clue about their ability to pay and what they are going to be like to work with.

## DON'T SEE ALL OTHER JOURNALISTS AS YOUR COMPETITION AT LEAST SOME OF THE TIME AND THINK OF THEM AS COLLEAGUES

A tough one this, for some, I know.

Yet the support of others who have chosen the same career path can be invaluable. Sites like JournoBiz, the forum at Journalism.co.uk or Joanne Mallon's Mediawomenuk group are frequented by people who will offer their time, kindness and experience to help you decide where you should pitch your next feature or how much to charge a commercial client. I've asked that very question more than once and have been set on the right track. What goes around, comes around. So long as you also offer advice and help where you can, then you will find membership (which is free but suggests voluntary contributions) worthwhile.

## FINDING MARKETS

This is another crucial element of successful freelancing and another one that seems to attract hogwash masquerading as advice. "Buy a writers' handbook", say some, "Get your hands on Media Disk", say others, "type writers wanted into Google and see what that brings you". These are all examples of some of the ways it's often suggested that you can find places to sell your work. And yes, they can help, just. But again, you must beware: books and disks go out of date very quickly, the 'writers wanted' positions are snapped up very quickly and might pay peanuts.

## WHAT ELSE CAN YOU DO?

It's pretty basic, if you ask me. Study the publications you want to write for, find out if they are open to freelancers, whether they pay, and how much, and, if you still want to, send them a pitch they can't say 'no' to. How difficult can that be? Oh, okay it's pretty difficult, but I do hope that reading this book might help you.

## KEEP GOING

One week, when I emailed four ideas to a section editor on a national newspaper, he came back and said that he "really wasn't interested" in the first, "couldn't care less" about the second, and declined to comment on the third. Luckily for me, he said the fourth sounded "interesting" so I kept in touch with him and filed 1,100 words. Another idea on a separate theme was also accepted a couple of days later.

Imagine all the ideas these people receive. Why on earth should they come back to you at all? They never asked you to get in touch. If you do get a curt "no", pick yourself up and have another go. If, on the other hand, you get: "It's not quite there for us, but do keep trying", then a dance around the room may be in order, not to mention dazzling them with another finely-tuned pitch that screams: "use me, use me".

## EDITORS: CAN'T LIVE WITH 'EM, CAN'T LIVE WITHOUT 'EM

Newsflash: editors are okay. They are human, they love their children. They might even have done their time as a freelance. If you are scared of editors, then don't be! (Go on, admit it, some people are; hard to believe, I know). Treat them with professional courtesy and respect and you should be okay. Reply to their queries, meet their deadlines, get their names right and don't let them down – what more could they ask?

But also remember, they need to do the same to you. I'm whispering now but some editors can be a tiny bit vague. They'll give you an unclear brief and expect you to calibrate your crystal ball to turn it into what they want. Some might even be – wait for it – difficult to please. They might ask for more and more until, frankly, you feel you may be losing the will to live.

I'll leave it up to you as to what you might want to do about working for them again.

## AND WHAT ABOUT THE WRITING?

As I said in my introduction, this is not a guide on how to write. You should find a much better means of finding that out before you have the brass neck to approach an editor to ask if they'd like to publish your work.

But I'll say this: keep it simple. Why use 50 words, when you can use 10? Why use five syllables when you can use two? Clear, concise copy is what counts, not how much irreverence, or how many clever words you can use per line. My training taught me that if someone had to read your intro twice to understand it, you've failed.

It sounds obvious, but how often can we say the stuff we read every day fulfils that oh-so-simple requirement?

## CHECK YOUR FACTS – THEN CHECK AGAIN

Research skills are vital. Make sure your references are sound. Just because something has already been published online or in print, it doesn't make it true. If someone is quoted as having an opinion, then contact them direct to check.

## REMEMBER: A DEADLINE ISN'T AN OPTIONAL EXTRA TEST

It's cardinal sin time. Repeat after me: "I will not miss my deadline, I will not miss my deadline, I will not miss my deadline". Okay, that's enough, you get the picture.

If you know in advance, through no fault of your own, that you might miss your deadline, then negotiate an extension. Otherwise, not only do you look like an idiot, you might not get work from that editor again. And what a shame that would be, especially when there are about 50 other would-be writers waiting to step into your shoes and who are perfectly capable of delivering on time.

## QUICK T!P

**WHERE ELSE CAN YOU FIND WRITING JOBS?**
I've listed some useful sites later on – to help in doing your own PR and also to suggest how you should respond to ads and word any entries you pay for on listings sites.

## THE NEXT STEP...

Take your time in planning where you go from here.

Think about what you want from your work and how you can balance it better with the rest of your life.

All the time, blood, sweat and tears you have spent, either in an unrelated career or as a regional journalist, may have left you exhausted (I know it did me). So think about what you want on your terms. Then work your hardest to find it.

You may not find an exact match, and yes times are tough, but there *is* still worthwhile work out there with your name on it.

# Advice from the Professionals

*" Write your first draft with your heart. Re-write with your head. "*

from Finding Forrester

# Chapter 2
# Advice from the Professionals

When you start a freelance writing career, it can seem an insurmountable challenge – look at who you are up against – these established writers have a wealth of experience and the by-lines to match.

You may feel you could never be that ubiquitous. But you could. While people like me trained years ago in what to write, how to interview, where, when, why and how, plenty more have chased a dream of earning a living from freelance writing and have made it a reality.

One such writer is Kelly Rose Bradford. You'll find her entertaining and provocative journalism in the Telegraph, Mail, Express and AOL's Parentdish, among other places.

Kelly believes that, although times are tight, if you are good enough, you will continue to get work as a freelance writer.

She worked in IT for five years, took redundancy, and used the money to establish herself as a freelancer. She also took a part time job as a library assistant for a couple of years to keep the money coming in. Kelly started off by writing fiction for women's magazines, trivia questions for arcade games and magazine's puzzle pages, and was then contracted to write a celebrity based quiz book. She says this was all fine – but she so wanted to write features…

## TIMES ARE DIFFERENT NOW

Kelly says that she wishes she'd found better advice when starting out.

"All the books I read were still telling would-be writers to send off completed articles and a self-addressed envelope. Initially, I knew no different. I had no other sources of information. There was very little advice out there, the internet was in its infancy as far as home-users went, and all my knowledge was coming from outdated books on How To Be a Journalist. Things changed for me once the web became the place to go for information.

"Things would have probably been different if I had been to university and knew about post-graduate courses in journalism and so on, but I didn't. I'd left school at 16, and to be honest, I thought newspaper contributors were all posh people with expensive education behind them and a relative in the editor's seat…

"Hindsight is a wonderful thing of course, but if I were 20 now, I'd probably try for an internship or do a recognised course. But I have no complaints, because I have come in via the backdoor and been very lucky – that's a synonym for hard work, dogged determination and pester power.

"I also wish I'd known a bit more about the legal side of things, and how soul-destroying and demanding working on real life features, involving complicated case studies, can be."

Kelly believes times have changed for the better.

"There is good, salient information out there now, and groups and societies you can join and make contacts and friends and find out about courses and so on.

"People are so much more aware of how the media works, too, and so it's easier to gain knowledge about how magazines and papers are put together."

Kelly's advice for new freelance writers:

- Have some cash behind you

- Network like crazy

- See a story in everything

- Read compulsively

- Keep ahead of trends

- Know what's going on

- Be reliable

- Be consistent

- Don't promise stuff you can't deliver

- Know what you're talking about

- Get a copy of McNae's

- Don't be gung-ho

- Or arrogant

- Or argue with editors over adds or amends

- See it as a business deal (You are doing this to make money, not to go into an artistic-integrity-meltdown because your opening paragraph has been meddled with)

Asked what she puts her success down to, Kelly makes some vital points.

She says: "I work very hard and remain ambitious. I see a story in everything. And I try very hard not to annoy people, that's important."

## DON'T GIVE UP

Writer and photographer Steve Newman is conscious of how freelance writing is becoming an increasingly crowded field. He says the guidance that will always ring true for him is "never give up."

He adds: "Study the publication first, at all times, before approaching a publication. Read your feature through twice after you have written it – and get someone else, your partner perhaps, to read it too.

"There are an awful lot more freelancers around now, far more than there used to be. So you must make sure you do everything right and do use social media to its full potential. Websites are still vitally important, no matter what others may say – blogs and Twitter even more so.

"You need to get yourself an online presence and get known, network with as many people as you can. Sites such as LinkedIn offer great opportunities."

Hannah Davies worked in publishing after dabbling in student journalism. She spent a year doing work experience, with the odd bit of paid work, living off savings.

She says she wishes she'd realised how hard it would be to freelance at the beginning; and that this is normal. Hannah reports that she had very few contacts and no confidence. When the commissions failed to appear, she says she thought it was because she was stupid.

But she adds: "I should have thought about it purely as a business – plenty of new ventures take a good few years to turn a profit, so a slow beginning doesn't mean you're doing something wrong, just that you have to put the time in before you see results.

"I also wish I'd gone on a freelance journalism course earlier than I did. Back then, I knew how to be a journalist, but I didn't know how to be a freelancer, and I didn't understand that I had this gap in my knowledge for about six months.

"My advice is that it takes time to build a freelance career. The most important advice I could offer would be to have a savings cushion at the very beginning – think of it as start-up capital for the business. And invest that capital wisely: perhaps a good freelancing course (ask around for recommendations, don't just go by the blurb), subscriptions to magazines or expert sourcing services, etc.

"I think it's very important to realise that writing is only a tiny part of being a successful freelance journalist (actually, that applies to all journalism, in my opinion): you need to be able to research, chase down case studies, conduct interviews, organise your time, deal with taxes, chase payments, network, market yourself.

"When I first started out, I met up with a fellow freelance writer who told me that she only spent about 10 per cent of her time actually writing. Back then, I assumed that meant she wasn't a very good freelance writer; now I know differently."

## FIND YOUR OWN WAY

Alex Gazzola is a respected freelance contributor on health and is a writing tutor. I never suspected Alex wasn't a trained journalist. But it transpires he worked in IT support and software training.

"This was the mid-90s, and I didn't know a single other writer, so there was no way of getting specific personal advice. I'd been doing a correspondence course, so there was always input from my tutor, but, as supportive as she was, a lot of the advice was quite general and, in hindsight, I can see that you really only learn on the job," says Alex.

"Part of me wants to say there was nothing that I wish I'd been advised – and in some ways I'm glad I had nobody to turn to because I had to learn from my mistakes and forge my own path through trial and error.

"In fact, I think my modest naivety probably even helped on occasion.

"But if I had to choose one thing, then I wish someone had told me that what I was doing – learning to sub-edit, writing for very modest or niche or average-paying magazines – was actually journalism and 'counted' as journalism.

"It seems silly now, but I didn't realise that it was. And I didn't realise, too, that writing for national papers or glossier magazines (which is what I considered proper journalism was) was a future possibility for me, and something I could work towards.

"I just didn't even consider it on my horizon, and wasted probably years not really being ambitious enough because of it."

Like Kelly, Alex is optimistic about what the future holds for freelance writers.

He says: "More people want to do it, and so, in some ways, it's more competitive. But in other ways, there are more opportunities as there is more media, and when there's more competition, it forces everyone to up their game – which is good for creativity and for forms of journalism in general."

## HARD LEARNED LESSONS

So what's Alex's advice for wannabe freelance writers?

"If you're really stuck and don't know how to move forward, then perhaps do a journalism course of some kind – but if you're quite savvy and fearless, then consider 'going it alone' – be self-taught," he says.

"Get to know other journalists, read a lot of books about journalism and writing, be nosy and curious, and be prepared to never stop learning.

"Don't feel disadvantaged if you don't have any qualifications or experience behind you. Enthusiasm and willingness to learn will carry you far."

According to Alex, the biggest misconception harboured at the start of a life as a freelance writer is that it's just writing. He says just 10 per cent of his working life is spent compiling pieces of work.

"I think some people fail, quite pitifully, to comprehend how many ideas they need to come up with," he adds. "They think they can be told what to write and then write it."

Anne Wollenberg writes about a variety of topics, including film and technology, and has an impressive portfolio of clients.

She says she wishes she'd been advised about managing her time and structuring her day.

"A lot of people think that, if they worked from home, they'd get nothing done. Actually, for a lot of freelancers, the problem is that they take on too much work, and they let the lines between home and work, and work and life, become all too blurred," says Anne.

"Have a designated area in which you do your work. Write down what you have to do, and how you've spent your time. You may be your own boss, but you still need to be answerable to someone – yourself."

Anne also offers important pointers about workload.

She adds: "Don't be afraid to say no. It's difficult, because you think you might never be asked again, and, every time you say no, you're turning down some extra cash, because, of course, you're not on a flat rate, you're paid for the work you do.

"But if you live to work rather than working to live, you'll eventually burn out. Be realistic about what you can take on. If you really hate saying no, you can always recommend another freelancer (if you know they're good enough to recommend) or outsource parts of your work, such as research.

"Always chase up pitches as that can result in a yes. Also, don't be snotty to people who've turned down your ideas or not replied. You never know when you might meet them again – or when they might dig out a year-old pitch and decide to commission it."

### ARE TIMES TOUGHER?

Anne says: "The general view is that times are tough for freelancers and there's less work and less money. I'm not convinced it's quite this clear-cut, as some companies have more money to spend on freelancers because of the fact that they've cut staff.

"For example, one company, having a recruitment freeze, has asked me to look after an entire magazine section. If you can cultivate good relationships, the current climate isn't actually all doom and gloom. There is still work to be had. And while some people would say there are more freelancers fighting over less work because so many people have been made redundant, the fact is that good freelancers are always hard to find, and the fact that there are more freelancers in general basically means editors are hunting for the same needle but in a bigger haystack, to use a lousy metaphor.

"There's never room to be complacent, but good freelancers should find that the work is out there.

"One thing notable about how things are now, though, is I'd say you should panic more quickly if you don't get paid. Don't let the unpaid invoices stack up and be very wary of new start-ups – ask for money upfront.

"Another way in which times have changed is that, three or four years ago, I would have recommended people do a journalism course, such as an NCTJ or postgrad. Now I'd say that potentially means gambling a large sum of money on a career that may not happen."

### TELLING IT LIKE IT IS: ADVICE FROM ANNE WOLLENBERG

- Speak to established freelancers and listen to what they say.

Anne says her experience is that people often ask advice and then get annoyed because they don't like what she has told them.

She explains: "You need to understand that the business you're going into is what it is – you can't make it the business you want it to be just by wishful thinking, you need to like it or lump it."

- Be polite and say thank you to everyone who helps you

"Other freelancers have said the same as me: even when you tell people this, very obviously stating that a big mistake is not to thank people for their advice, you still get no reply," says Anne. "Which is stupid, not because you need to be fawning over people in gratitude, but because it is always worth trying to cultivate good relationships. You never, ever know when someone might need help, or cross over to being an editor. And be prepared to work at it – the work is not just going to fall into your lap, however much you think it should or hope it would."

## SHOULD ASPIRING WRITERS STILL BOTHER?

Anne says:

"Think carefully about it. Anyone wanting to become self-employed by choice, as in quitting a job rather than having been thrown into it by redundancy, should have some savings. If you're starting a business, it is common sense to save first. You may not make any money to begin with.

"I'd only tell them not to bother if they thought they would be writing for the Sunday Times and Marie Claire within a week and did not expect to live hand-to-mouth for a bit or to have to plan ahead or cut down on luxuries."

What does Anne put her success down to?

She says: "I'm not sure, really. Luck, a knack for the whole thing, hard graft, more luck. I always meet deadlines.

"I have a good rapport with my clients, who then recommend me to other people. I think it's doing really obvious things: doing what I'm asked to do, when I'm asked to do it. Because, as those who work on the staff side know, it's much harder than you might think to find reliable freelancers.

"Good writers and subeditors who do what they are asked to do are actually like gold dust. I do simple things that should be a given – read the style guide, read the publication. You wouldn't believe how many people don't. It's a sad fact that I think I am successful just because I do my job properly."

And what has been her biggest source of help?

"Other freelancers, without a shadow of a doubt," says Anne.

"They are the people who know who is commissioning and can recommend you to other people. An unbelievable amount of my work comes through word of mouth. Other freelancers are not the enemy, they are the competition but are also your colleagues, so think about how you treat them."

## LESSONS LEARNED QUICKLY

Former civil servant Emily Carlisle is a blogger, feature writer, consultant and aspiring novelist. Her professional writing website is at **www. allaboutemily.com** and her award-winning blog is More than just a mother: **www.morethanjustamother.com**

At the time of writing, she is around six months into a freelance writing career but she feels she has learned some lessons very quickly.

Emily says: "It hasn't been an easy thing to do, although, when I look back to where I was six months ago, I've come a long way. I rather like the challenge of breaking into an industry in which I have no contacts or experience, but it's hard work and I suspect it'll be a long time before I'll feel secure.

"I've already learned how vital it is to get the pitch right, how important networking is, and to develop a thick skin.

"Speaking to editors on the phone instead of sending chase-up emails has worked well for me. Even where this hasn't resulted in a commission, each conversation has taught me something new about that editor, or about the publication."

And what hasn't worked so well?

"When I first started out, I had a rather scattergun approach – pitching left, right and centre and not getting anywhere," says Emily.

"As soon as I settled into more of a specialism, my approach gained focus and I began seeing results.

"I've found it reassuring to discover that some extremely successful freelance journalists are career-changers themselves, and I've also found that the majority of journalists are supportive to others.

"That said, it's also become clear to me how many freelance writers are trying to make a living in what are very tough times, so I know I need to be the best I possibly can be if I want to succeed."

## MISTAKES INEXPERIENCED FREELANCE WRITERS MAKE

Most freelance writers will admit to mistakes made along the way. Mine included not being confident enough sometimes in approaching editors, and letting commissions slip because of it. I should have kept in touch better with editors to make sure my work saw the light of day. There's more on effectively following up pitches in chapter five.

I asked some veteran freelancers what mistakes they felt newer writers made. If you can aim to avoid similar pitfalls in the early days of your writing career, this could help you prosper:

Alex Gazzola from Mistakes Writers Make (And How to Put Them Right) **http://mistakeswritersmake.blogspot.co.uk/**:

Being too interested in yourself rather than other people.

I know some people make a living from selling their lives, but most of us go looking for stories well away from home.

I think the internet, Twitter/Facebook, blogging and social media has allowed everyone to put their voice and opinion in the public domain, and I think somewhere along the line this has become a bit blurred with journalism.

New wannabes think their opinion is what matters in journalism, and that their opinion will change everything and revolutionise the world.

'I can't wait to tell everyone what I think!' is something that makes my heart sink when I hear it from a wannabe. Few people care what you think. Readers care about what they think, and they mostly read to learn, not to read the opinion of someone they've never heard of.

Also:

- Ruling out swathes of potential markets because 'they're just not me' or 'I don't know anything about yachts / horses / cement / whatever'. So what? Research. It's your job.

- Forgetting it's a business. You have to be prepared to talk money and not get embarrassed.

- Thinking copyright doesn't matter. It matters to you, to fellow writers, and to the publishing business. You owe it to yourself and the writing community to understand the basics.

*How can they get over these?*

By cultivating an obsessive interest with everything and everyone else. If you're not interested in the world, and in asking questions and obtaining answers, then you are in very serious trouble, and I'm not sure anyone is in a position to help you.

Editor and writer Sarah Drew Jones:
**www.malthusmedia.co.uk/**

- Failing to live up to the promise of the original pitch, or veering wildly away from it. Some people are just great pitchers, but not good writers or researchers, maybe…
Terrible spelling, grammar, punctuation and syntax bloopers. I hate it when writers don't check the basics before filing. My personal favourite? Random Caps in Sentences: I will never understand this.

What on earth Are they Thinking? There's Something about It that makes me Want to kill Somebody, very Slowly.

- Attaching the invoice when they file the piece (unless specifically asked to do so). It's so presumptuous…
  I'm not a fan of freelancers who argued (I remember one would-be contributor coming back to me a week after I'd turned down his pitch, asking if I'd re-consider it as it just seems so right and then attaching the exact same pitch again).
  Freelancers emailing asking 'what are you working on right now? What can I help with?'. This is fine if it's a regular relationship, but when it's clearly a random email – probably a round robin one to tens of editors, too, it's pointless and annoying.

Cathy Winston, editor and freelance journalist. Former lifestyle editor, Fabulous magazine
**www.cathywinston.com**

- Missing deadlines has to come top. It's astonishing how many people think it's a vague guideline. I had one freelancer who was so hard to get hold of that I ended up having to find out additional information I needed myself when she didn't get back to me. She eventually replied after the magazine had gone to press. Then asked if I'd commission her again.

- Not being on word count. I don't mean hitting it bang on, but the person who filed just over 2,500 words for a 1,000 word feature, and said she didn't know what to cut, never got commissioned again. 1,200/1,300 words was fine as sometimes you'd need more, and it saved adds, but that just seemed so lazy.

- People telling me what I should commission when they pitched. It's a fine line between 'I thought this would work well for xxx page' (fine – shows they've researched it) and 'this idea is perfect for you' (well, actually, that's my decision).

- People who argue after you've turned down the pitch. It may not even have always been my decision to say no (editors have editors remember) but regardless, you aren't getting it reversed. You are, however, annoying me. A lot.

- People who didn't do any research about the magazine. I wouldn't expect people to know exactly what we might want to use, but pitching for the such and such page when that doesn't exist is annoying.

Anne Wollenberg:
**www.annewollenberg.co.uk**

Being freelance is actually much, much harder than people imagine.

I think the biggest sin is not following briefs and not seeing them for what they are. They are customer order forms! Also, not reading the style guide and the publication, and therefore filling the word count with inappropriate content. If readers will be familiar with a concept, don't spend a paragraph explaining it. If the magazine is for a family audience, don't make rude jokes.

Another one is not being around to answer questions after filing. You may be irritated by subeditors coming to you with questions after you file but, like it or not, it is always going to be your fault for not checking your facts or not making something clear or not asking a question you should have. If you're not going to be around, have the courtesy to let the publication know and put an out-of-office reply on your email. I have had writers completely ignore queries after filing – perhaps thinking the sub is just annoying them and will go away if ignored.

Which brings me to my next mistake: not respecting production staff. A lot of writers find queries irritating. And a lot of writers also make the mistake of thinking that subs sit in a separate department and wield no power. Subeditors and production editors tend to work closely with senior staff and they know what your copy was like before it was edited. It's not clever to annoy them. If you aren't around to answer questions, or your copy is a mess, they can and will stop you from getting further commissions. I find some writers are very contemptuous towards subs. It's really not clever.

Also not clever is refusing to do anything that's not in your commission. Sure, you might ask for some extra cash if you're asked to do a lot of extra research. But, before now, I've had writers snap: "That wasn't in my commission" when they've been asked to, say, make one suggestion for what kind of picture might work. You need to remember that you are running a business and what you need to do is offer decent customer service. You serve editors, not the other way round – don't be a doormat, but do find a balance.

The other mistake is being precious. If I ever hear one more person complain about having their perfectly-crafted text edited, because they haven't comprehended that all text needs a bit of editing to make it fit and that what they're doing is not an art form, I will scream. It doesn't matter if things got cut or changed. Live with it. If you want to be precious, you're in the wrong job.

I know this from being on the other side, in various staff jobs and freelance positions. You write a clear brief asking them to include X and Y, and not to include Z, only for this to be ignored. I think people sometimes believe that, because writing is (they think) something creative, the brief is a creative jumping-off point. It's no more acceptable to ignore the brief or change it without speaking to your editor first than it would be for you to order soup in a restaurant and be served ice-cream instead. I think people fail to see a brief like an order form and think following it is optional.

It's also surprisingly difficult to find freelancers who will tell you if something goes wrong rather than waiting until the deadline day to let you know. Standards matter hugely, because the reason for hiring a freelancer is to get something done quickly and easily. You don't have time to do it in-house, or it's a bit of a hassle to do, so you farm it out. It should be blindingly obvious that what you ask for is what you want to get.

I think people also fail to understand the entire process – they don't understand that, after they file, the copy has to be laid out, subbed and fitted, and so on. I once had a freelancer assume that because the publication was going to press and we wouldn't process their copy, it was fine to file it late. It wasn't fine, and, if they'd asked, we could have told them that.

I have heard editors say again and again that you'd think it would be easy to do what you are asked, yet so many freelancers don't. Nobody likes being messed around by, say, their gas company or their phone company. It's not okay for you to mess your clients around, either.

The hardest thing of all, though, is finding subeditors. I have hired freelance subeditors with outstanding CVs who have turned out to be useless. Which is why, if you want to get into subbing, you shouldn't get the hump if you're asked to do one trial shift (so long as you are paid for it). I would never again risk hiring a sub without a trial run. I find it astonishing the number of people who don't read the style guide, don't listen to what they're told, don't take notes (so they ask the same questions again and again), leave widows and orphans in text, and generally just don't do the job properly. Some have let slip very early on that they've exaggerated on their CVs.

As a freelance sub, I read the style guide, read the publication and take notes so I never have to ask the same question twice. It's not rocket science, yet so few people do this. The other thing they fail to do is read adverts. If the advert says you need to work in-house and be able to use InDesign, don't ask to do it remotely and say you don't know InDesign but could learn.

After reading these mistakes, and things to be learned, you may have a fair idea of how to not annoy an editor.

## YOU HAVEN'T HEARD IT ALL

The final word goes to two freelance writers/editors who have put forward mistakes you may be forgiven for thinking could never happen – but they do. Tina's and Lynley's examples of people not doing their job properly may offer you some hope – that you could never make such a basic mistake!

Make sure you research who to contact and don't insult your editor…

Tina Walsh:
www.tina-walsh.com/

Tina is a journalist and copywriter of 20 years' standing.

A freelancer got in touch through my website and said she'd love me to commission her for [a publication] and could she send some ideas over. Only problem was, I wasn't an editor there.

Lynley Oram
http://www.lynley.org/

Lynley has worked as a senior editor on various magazines, often connected with computers.

Don't insult the editor in your pitch. Please. It is surprising how many would say something like "your coverage of this area is dreadful, you need someone to do it properly. Here is my idea". Why? Why tell the editor of a section that something they're doing is rubbish? How is that going to make them want to hire you?

## SIX OF THE BEST: MISTAKES FREELANCE WRITERS MAKE

1.  Not researching the publication properly

2.  Not fulfilling the brief

3.  Ignoring the style guide

4.  Not including all relevant details

5.  Showing their irritation at being asked to add more to copy already filed

6.  Wasting an editor's time

# The Business
# of Freelancing

*" It is impossible to discourage the real writers – they don't give a damn what you say, they're going to write. "*

Sinclair Lewis

# Chapter 3
# The Business of Freelancing

Ask yourself:

Can I afford to go freelance?

Tot up your monthly outgoings on the mortgage, bills, food and other essentials. If you have the contacts, experience and drive, not to mention work lined up to match or exceed this total, then go for it. But still proceed with caution. Even the most successful freelancers might have a rocky start.

In my first month as a freelancer, in 1999, I earned £160. The next, a little more. For the next 12 months, feast and famine set in, with earnings some months at around £7,000, but mostly at £1,500-£2,500. And some months I didn't crack £1,000.

I was in the lucky position of having a partner on a modest wage and also had the small matter of two young children to look after – that's why I could afford to go freelance – because we took the attitude that whatever I earned, amid looking after the kids, was a "bonus" and we were prepared to make sacrifices.

If you think you are going to rake in the cash weeks into a freelance career, then think again. We got by because entertaining two little girls doesn't cost much. "Feeding the ducks is free", I'd say, as we set off for the park, and it also happens to be a great inspiration for flogging some features.

**A TAXING MATTER**

Go and see your local tax office before you file your first piece and make sure you are doing everything right. Look into tax and national insurance. I am not a tax inspector nor am I an accountant, but I can tell you that if you put off doing this, then you could be sorry (I was, thanks to a £100 fine for not sorting it soon enough). Resources for the right advice when setting up a new business are at the back of this book.

Find out all about what expenses you can claim for as costs for your writing business – office rent, travel, some equipment and consumables, plus money spent on training and any marketing.

You may want to talk to an accountant about what's best for you – should you work as a sole trader or set up as a limited company (some freelancers do, but this is likely to be further down the road). Also, find out as much as you can about whether you want to fill in an annual self assessment form, do it online or pay an accountant to do it. Of course, if money is tight then you will want to do it yourself, but I know plenty of freelancers who have commissioned the services of an accountant to save time and peace of mind. You should also ask all about registering for VAT. This is compulsory if you have a turnover above a certain threshold (At the time of going to press, £73,000) but it may also be of benefit if you earn less than that – seek sound advice on this. But remember, if you do voluntarily register for VAT, you will still have to follow all the rules that someone who has had to register must also stick to.

## TRAINING COURSES

The popular **www.journalism.co.uk** website has a calendar of training courses on various aspects of writing and journalism. Individual authors and journalists run their own workshops or training courses. Companies such as the Writers Bureau oversee correspondence courses. National journalists Olivia Gordon and Johanna Payton hold sessions aimed at 'real life' magazine and newspaper journalism. I also run workshops on making more money. The BBC has a training wing and, of course, the NUJ has a schedule of training to keep you up to date with latest practises within journalism. If you're embarking on a professional writing career, find out about such opportunities and fathom which is best for you.

## SHOW ME THE MONEY

Ask yourself, should I write for free?

Midlands author, writing courses creator and well-known writing forum **www.mywriterscircle.com** founder Nick Daws illustrates a point often raised by freelancers.

He says: "I've always avoided writing for free. Writers should be paid a fair wage and those who routinely work for free are effectively undercutting those of us who depend on writing for our livelihood.

"I recently did a small job to allow a company to assess my style and I could assess what the job would involve. I wouldn't adopt this approach for anything more substantial. I might be willing to accept a lower than usual fee for writing say, a test article, if I genuinely believed it was going to lead on to better things. I'd definitely expect payment if the job was going to take me more than half a day or so.

"You need to judge any offer carefully. If it's just a small job to test your skills, and you're confident it could lead to regular work, go for it. But if it's more substantial, be prepared to negotiate. Point out to the editor that this will take a fair bit of work and, as a professional writer, you expect some recompense. If they are reasonable people, they should understand and accept this. If not, you're probably better off not working for them anyway."

While some writers will tell you writing for free definitely helps lead to paid work, others urge caution for different reasons. One told me: "Beware of any editors offering 'jam tomorrow,' saying if you write for free now, when their publication becomes successful, they'll start paying you. What often happens is that, if the publication takes off, they'll dump you and hire some higher-profile, established journalist. Writing for free is fine at the very beginning – for college and local publications, say – but always bear in mind that you're building a career."

That last point is key – even if you choose to write for free in the early days. Is the site and your work going to count for anything on a CV if the site, itself, is a bit shoddy?

Would you expect a plumber or mechanic to do their job for free? No? So why do publishers instruct aspiring journalists to submit their finely crafted features without any pay? Ask any new writers and they'll tell you how difficult it is to 'crack' that elusive vicious circle; you want a job, editors want experience. You pitch a feature; they want evidence of a track record – cuttings of already published work.

So what can you do? Writing for free is a harmless way of proving you have what it takes, isn't it? Well no, actually. You must beware – for every publication offering you exposure as your sole reward, there are plenty more experienced hacks who'll tell you to tread carefully.

### ARE YOU BEING RIPPED OFF?

Ask yourself "Is this publication ripping me off or do they genuinely have a limited budget?" If so, why? If they can't afford to pay their writers, why is this, and do you really want to write for them?

Weigh up if the piece will genuinely have the possibility of leading to other work, building a specialism or boosting your reputation.

Be prepared to ask for a fee if a job is going to take a lot of work. Ask for expenses at the very least.

Do you care passionately about the issue you are reporting on? Will it make a genuine difference? (And even then, some would say "remember, the resulting warm glow doesn't pay the bills").

## MORE ON RIGHTS AND COPYRIGHT

"Help, an editor has stolen my idea!" Stop right there. What a coincidence – your idea about a calendar for crafts activities has been nicked by a major publishing house. What nonsense! You can guarantee that the day Victoria Beckham gives a nod to her latest thoughts on health or family, there'll be plenty of writers – staff and freelance – who'll be attempting to sell a piece on 'ordinary' women with the same concerns. Except yours, of course, they'll call it a 'case study'.

Read this and remember it, pin it up on your fridge (or your computer monitor might be a better idea, sorry) if you like: There is no copyright on an idea.

If you do happen to spot a feature in a magazine or newspaper that you reckon looks 'similar' to something you suggested, then either congratulate yourself on having the right sort of thought processes or have a word with yourself about being too obvious. But don't spend a minute stressing over what might have been.

Who says they weren't already working on the piece before you came along? Who says another freelance didn't suggest the same idea, someone who already has an 'in' with the editor?

Of course, there are exceptions to every rule, but that's my story and I'm sticking to it.

And no, I'm not saying that because I've nicked anyone's ideas!

There's a great guide – 10 Things Every Freelance Should Know About Copyright – available through the National Union of Journalists.

## CONTRACTS: READ THE SMALL PRINT

When you are commissioned to write a piece for a newspaper, magazine, or website, you should be asked to sign a contract or agree to the terms of the job. You must check the small print carefully. Some places will be happy to take on work on a "second rights" basis, others will insist on "first rights", while an increasing number expect you to pass over "all rights," something the National Union of Journalists has something to say about! This is from the NUJ: "What you sell to an editor is a license to use your work, once, in one territory, in one medium. Examples are First British Serial Rights and World Wide Web Reprint Rights."

In every case, read the contract carefully. Otherwise, it will come as a shock to you when your carefully crafted prose pops up in another magazine or newspaper – without an extra penny coming your way. Raise any queries with the editor or seek advice about how you might be able to challenge the "rights grab".

## PLEASE SIR, CAN I HAVE SOME MORE?

"I'm so rubbish at asking for more pay." "How can I get more money, I don't want to tick off my editor."

If ever either of these sentiments begin to figure in your way of thinking, then it's time to take action. You can ask and sometimes you will get more money. Believe in yourself and your abilities, but don't ask for trouble.

For example, some newspapers will tell you what their rates are. Even then, you can treat them as the minimum payment to expect, so there is no harm in a polite enquiry as to whether they can be improved. If you have turned a piece around under exceptional circumstances, such as getting hold of someone who would never usually speak to the media, or you have stepped in after another writer has let the editor down, then rates could be negotiable.

Whatever the fee, make sure you know it when you accept the commission. That way, nobody can pull the wool over your eyes (as if they would!) and you know where you stand.

Within reason, you can always negotiate. What have you got to lose? No editor worth their salt is going to think you are pushy if you do so, so long as you are in a position of strength, and, in my humble opinion, that means you have a brilliant story and you supply great copy.

Sometimes a client will ask you what you will charge. When this happens, I ask them what budget is available, or I name a price based on various factors – how major is the publication, how good is the story, how much work will it take? And, possibly the most important, how big is the PITA factor? That's Pain in the A*** if anyone is wondering.

The NUJ runs Pitch and Deal courses, which are open to members and non-members alike. They also publish an excellent Rate for the Job guide, but again, they stress that these fees can be treated as the minimum.

If you are writing for newspapers and magazines, you also need to be kind to yourself and your pockets by applying for ALCS (Authors' Licensing and Collecting Society) payments. This brings royalty payments for a range of ways your articles may be reused, including photocopying in some libraries. Don't assume yours won't be included. This trusted body shares out millions of pounds to deserving writers. Make sure you get what you are due.

## CHASING PAYMENT

Start at the beginning. Ask your editor who to invoice when you are commissioned, or get in touch with the accounts department of the publication that has accepted your article and ask them how they pay. Make sure you know when to invoice – some people send an invoice with their feature, if that's what's expected, but some editors will take umbrage at this. Don't be scared of asking to make sure you can get it right.

What information do they need on the invoice to process it quickly? Find out the name of the person you'll need to speak to in accounts, plus their direct line and email address.

Accounts departments like the easy alternative and, if your invoice has all the relevant information on it, the more likely you are to get paid on time. So that means:

- Name

- Address

- Phone Number

- Email details

- Date

- Work completed, number of words, for which edition

- Your own reference number or code

- Any purchase order information or reference number assigned by the commissioning editor

- Terms and conditions of payment

Ask when they need your invoice by to ensure the most prompt payment.

If the expected payment date comes and goes, and no money appears, ring your named contact and ask when you can expect the payment. If days turn into weeks, send a statement. After this, within reason, ring or email regularly. Please don't hold back on this – that's your money they're holding on to. And what's more, you can charge interest if the client hasn't paid up according to your terms.

Freelance journalist Louise Bolotin has written a detailed guide to chasing payments and this is published at the JournoBiz forums. You can find further guidance at **www.journalism.co.uk**

Louise recommends The Better Payment Practice Campaign (**www.payontime.co.uk**) which contains everything you need to know to chase a debt and is written in clear and concise language. There's a calculator to work out how much interest and compensation you are owed, as well as sample Letters before action and agreements to accept payment by instalment.

When you are starting out, I know how stressful this sounds. The bad news is that it really is. People who give up freelancing may be perfectly good at it, when it comes to writing and selling their services. But dreaded cash flow problems can sink even the busiest freelancers. Such headaches can also keep you awake at night and I should know. Do yourself a favour and get to grips with this stuff as soon as you can, it could make or break your freelance success. Be as businesslike and meticulous as you can.

## A KILLER BLOW

You're not supposed to accept a smaller fee if your commissioned piece isn't published.

A kill fee may be offered if your feature doesn't see the light of day.

Some papers over-commission and much content is ordered but never carried. There are dozens of writers chasing payment on pieces that never saw the light of day. If you met your brief, you should be paid in full. End of. That's the theory. Check out what the NUJ has to say on this important matter. But, of course, it's not always like that – find out the publication's policy on 'kill fees' before you write for them. If you don't like it, you might want to reconsider.

If you haven't met your brief then you might have to accept a kill fee, but not before they've given you a chance to get it right.

I have accepted a kill fee twice and probably got more stressed about having done so than I would have by finding the courage to ask for the full amount.

Your head (and bank balance) tells you: "You must say no, go on, tell them you want the full amount," while your heart (and a little nagging voice) counters: "Hang on, I'd love to work for this editor again," or "I'm not actually feeling that assertive today."

So what can you do?

While freelancing for women's magazines, Catherine Cooper found that certain types of story "crash" so often that there's no point asking for a kill fee for time spent on a piece if that falls through. But if you have filed before the proverbial hits the fan, you can and should still ask for your fee.

"If I wrote an article and it wasn't used for no reason other than they had decided not to use it, even though it was up to scratch, in house style and so on, I would expect the whole fee," says Catherine. "I've written a couple of pieces which, to my knowledge, have never been used, and have still been paid, without having to negotiate a kill fee. I wouldn't write for a market that was in the habit of regularly killing pieces for no good reason. If I do the work, I expect to be paid."

Cooper adds that part of the reason real life stories pay so well is because of their sensitive nature, the case studies tend to be volatile. "It's just a risk with that kind of writing," she says.

But Rachael Glazier, from the Brighton and mid-Sussex branch of the NUJ, advises you shouldn't take a kill fee, as she believes strongly that this has a negative impact on other freelancers.

"Editors need to be reminded that kill fees are not acceptable," she says. "Every time someone accepts a kill fee, it undermines the efforts of other journalists and the unions to ensure that we are paid a proper wage for the work done, not the work published.

"I know that when money's tight, or you are starting out, it is tempting to take whatever you can get, but I think it's a short-term solution. Can you really afford to keep taking half of what you agreed to be paid for your work? And just because you may be able to, can your colleagues afford to work with that kind of uncertainty hanging over them?

"No one wants to lose a regular client, but is it worth your while to continue working for someone who may pay you less than you agreed?"

Rachael advises freelancers facing this issue to look for other work. "I've had one editor reduce my fee because she decided to cut a piece for space reasons," she says. "I pointed out that this wasn't acceptable, got the original fee and never pitched to her again. Life's too short and there are other markets out there. Be polite and move on if necessary."

## A REAL LIFE APPROACH

A blogger once contacted me with the following question:

Is a desire to write and a willingness to throw your hand at anything enough?

My answer was, of course, no.

You need to know that the craft of writing may not be the most important factor in getting paid for it. An ability to meet deadlines, interviews and research skills are equally important and, for some, more important.

If you are serious about earning money from writing for newspapers, magazines and websites, take the time to learn how best to do it. Invest in training, read, read and read some more, the publications or sites you want to write for, in particular. Find out if they even have a freelance budget. Learn about which laws govern what you can and can't write. Join forums where you can get frank feedback on your efforts from professionals. Subscribe to services and magazines that explain more about writing, journalism and what opportunities are out there.

Use social media the best you can to build relationships, find information and make the most of opportunities that could help progress a writing career.

There are plenty of established freelance writers struggling to get commissions and money in their pocket so, for a new potential contributor to stand out from the crowd, boy do they need to get it right. Do not pitch high paying or high profile markets until you are absolutely sure you can deliver. There is much more to writing for a living than 'throwing your hand to it.'

To anyone reading this who thinks I may be coming across as a little harsh, then I'm sorry, I don't mean to be – it's just, as far as I am concerned, now more than ever, anyone trying to earn money from freelance writing needs to be realistic about the way to go about it. For some, at the moment, the 'correct' answer to all of these queries would be: 'Want to be a freelance writer? Don't bother.'

## IF YOU HAVE CHILDREN

For many parents, a freelance career is a dream. To keep the dream alive, you have to be realistic about your prospects, how much work you can manage and how it really fits with the demands of a family.

It's sometimes impossible to know who can be the most unpredictable – customers or children.

Which one would you banish to the naughty step, if you really had the choice? The little mite who lets slip a rude word or the client who moves the goalposts so far from your original brief, you begin to question your ability to understand your mother tongue.

Even the most meticulously planned childcare arrangements can go to pot when a call comes through, as your youngest is on the potty or an unexplained rash puts you in the doctor's waiting room.

## WHERE CAN YOU START?

First off, I'd say take a long hard look at the hours you really can work.

Expecting too much of yourself, and nurturing a wildly over ambitious financial target, is a recipe for disaster and, potentially, a nervous breakdown.

## SETTING YOUR HOURS

Antonia Chitty, author of *Family Friendly Working* (White Ladder Press, 2008) says it's important to take a business-like approach to freelancing from the start.

"Set yourself some realistic working hours," she says. "Build in breaks and make it a strict rule to turn off the computer at the end of your work period.

"It's all too easy to end up burnt out. Obviously, there are always exceptional deadlines, but if you can keep work for weekdays and evenings and weekends to relax, you will feel better and work more effectively too."

Media coach Joanne Mallon agrees. She says: "It's easy to get sucked into working way more than you ever would if you were on staff. Decide how you work best and feel free to change your hours when you need to, this is one of the perks of being your own boss. Are you a morning, afternoon or evening person? Do you need to go out on the school run?"

## SEPARATING 'HOME' AND 'WORK'

I found out early on that expecting a would-be client to come to my home, littered as it was with wonky naked Barbies and remnants of mashed up chicken stuck in the skirting board wasn't the best plan.

Joanne has some excellent, practical advice to help you avoid the hell that can be caused by lack of organisation.

She says: "File work-related books and paperwork on a high shelf children can't reach. Always keep plenty of printer paper, as children will steal this for 'projects'.

"Make sure that your family and friends know that you are actually working and are not always available to run errands or chat on the phone.

"Teach your children, from an early age, that they are to be quiet when you're on the phone.

"They'll get the message eventually, though they may still want to sit on your knee while you're talking.

"Many freelancers find that Very Important Phone calls tend to coincide with their child's bowel movements, so don't be surprised if you're interrupted by a child waving something pretty revolting at you – revolting for the client that is, you'll possibly think that as long as they're quiet, it doesn't matter."

And in these days of social media networking, Joanne advises making sure you're not clogging up professional channels of communication with personal trivia.

She says: "Have separate email accounts and, if possible, a separate phone line. If you use Facebook and Twitter, think about whether you're going to be in 'home' or 'work' mode and whether you want them to overlap. Do you really want your clients seeing your latest holiday snaps?"

## DEALING WITH FAMILY EMERGENCIES

It's stressful enough telling one boss you can't come into work because your toddler son has food poisoning, telling the three people you were supposed to be working for in one day is even harder.

But Antonia says that one of the great upsides of freelancing is that you can drop everything if you need to – and pick it up again later.

She says: "Trouble is, you end up working into the small hours to catch up."

Joanne adds: "We can never totally plan for emergencies, but there's no harm in having a back-up plan. Who would be your emergency childcare? Who could you outsource work to if you needed to?

"One sure thing about life is that the unexpected will always occur, whether you're freelance or not. Don't waste too much time worrying about what hasn't happened yet, and trust in your ability to deal with whatever life chucks at you."

## FOR PARENTS AND NON-PARENTS

### Should you get an office?

I did. People asked me how I could afford it. I said I couldn't afford not to. The carnage wrought by toddler twins was no breeding ground for a successful career.

Antonia adds: "It's ideal if you can have a separate workspace. Depending on how noise resistant you are, you may need a desk in the corner, a separate room or even a garden office.

"Make sure you have space for records and filing. I like to have a bookshelf for work books, too. Because my children are younger, I actually do a lot of work in the centre of the home, and I'm used to punching out quick replies to emails and writing in short bursts. This doesn't work for every project, so I save indepth research for when the kids are out. I do have an office, though, where I can leave papers and ongoing projects out.

"If you're thinking of renting an office, think about the pros and cons. It is lovely to have a clear office space, but it can make a great difference to your business finances. Your earnings now have to cover rent every month.

"If you find working from home an isolating experience, a shared office is ideal. Do visit a few times to see the office in full swing, though, to find out whether your desk would be next to a loud sales person. And if freelancing is just the start of grand business ideas, you should incorporate the cost of office rates and insurance."

## TIME MANAGEMENT IS KEY

Joanne says: "Freelancers can be such procrastinators – I call it the freelancer's dance, when you mess about for ages and end up only just about hitting your deadline.

"It's very easy to feel you are being pulled in all directions, and that no-one is getting the best of you. Do not use every time your child starts to play as an opportunity to check your emails – actually get down and play with them and give them your 100% attention."

Antonia adds: "One of the big ups of freelancing is the chance to take time off during the week, to go for a swim when the pool is at its emptiest or meet a mate for a long lunch.

"But to do this and still have money to pay for it, you need to plan ahead. Work out how much you need to earn each month to pay your bills and have spending money.

"Allow for tax and National insurance, too. You might wonder what this has to do with time management… but time is money. Your income will depend on the hours you put in."

Nick Daws adds: "My favourite tip is to write a 'To Do' list first thing in the morning, prioritize what needs doing, then work steadily through the list, completing the highest priority tasks first. I'm also a strong believer in focusing on one task at a time until you have completed it. I advise setting aside blocks of time (say 30 minutes) for the task in question, and, during these sessions, not allow yourself to be distracted by anything short of fire or nuclear attack. The Pomodoro Technique (**www.pomodorotechnique. com**) provides a more formalised version of this method."

## WORK-LIFE BALANCE: WHAT TO DO ABOUT HOLIDAYS?

When freelance education journalist Janet Murray planned to take the summer off, she worried about how much work this would lose her.

"Because my workload is unpredictable, I go through periods that are very intense," she says. "In my case, with a small child and part-time childcare, that might mean a couple of weeks of very late nights and early mornings, working over the weekend to get things done. As a result, I reach a point where I need a break. But I fret about it a lot."

To help make her break possible, she stopped pitching, set a date to stop working, and planned to stick to it. Sounds simple, doesn't it?

But we all know it's not.

"Sod's law means you always get your best opportunities a week before you're due to go on holiday or take a break, so you have to work like mad before you go," says Janet.

You may have a nagging doubt about missing work. Don't put the rest of your life on hold for work.

Make sure clients and contacts are aware of when you'll be away.

Full-time blogger, Amber McNaught says she finds the time leading up to holidays, a "physical and mental strain" and that she always takes her laptop with her.

"By the time I leave for my holiday, I'm always utterly exhausted – then I worry that when I come home I'll have to live on beans on toast for a while because my income will have dried up. I often wonder if it's worth all the hassle, but luckily it always is."

Amber writes a couple of non-time-dependent articles every week, which she then files away for future use.

"By the time I need to take a break, I have enough posts written to keep things ticking over while I'm gone," she says. "It's not ideal, because I can only write certain types of articles in advance, but it helps to take some of the stress out of going away."

# Writing for Newspapers and Magazines

*" Everything in life is writable about if you have the outgoing guts to do it, and the imagination to improvise. The worst enemy to creativity is self-doubt. "*

Sylvia Plath

# Chapter 4
# Writing for Newspapers and Magazines

I said in my introduction that this is not a guide on how to write. That would be a whole volume in itself. I have listed some useful resources later on to help you learn more. As a new freelance writer, you have to realise that there are certain styles and conventions to follow to make sure you work again.

You can have all the pitching gumption in the world, and get your approach to an editor as fine-tuned as you like, but if you can't deliver on what you promise in your pitch, it's likely you won't be able to darken that editor's doorstep again.

Here's some brief guidance on how to give it your best shot when writing for newspapers or magazines.

## POINTS TO REMEMBER

Freelancing for these demanding customers is about far more than being able to string a sentence together.

I've mentored people over the years who seem convinced that an ability to craft perfect prose is all they need to master to satisfy even the most demanding of editors. It simply isn't so. You can write as nicely as you like but if you haven't got all the facts, that's what's going to trip you up.

Research skills are just as important, if not more so. These are explored in chapter six.

Make sure your news story, opinion piece, feature, or whatever else you are submitting, is as strong as it can be. Take a step back and play devil's advocate. Are you telling your readers everything that really matters? Or have you missed out any crucial information that would make the story more compelling, easy to follow or important? If you can genuinely answer this questions with a 'no', make sure you haven't buried that vital point too far into the story.

## INCLUDE BASIC INFORMATION

I mean people's names, ages, jobs, addresses, and so on – depending on what the house style of your publication is. People much cleverer than me will argue about whether the fact that someone is a mother or has been divorced, say, is relevant to some stories, but you shouldn't forget that often these details *are* needed to help your readers get a fuller picture. If you put them in, production staff can edit where needed, but if you leave them out, that means a lot more work for your editor, who has to find you and ask you.

In both news and features, editors need to see that all the relevant facts are there.

At a most basic level, that means if you are writing about a woman in a women's magazine feature, for example, you need to include:

- Your subject's name

- Your subject's job/former job, if they are a stay-at-home mum

- Her age

- If she has a husband or partner, their name, occupation and age

- Any children's names and ages

- Where they live, expressed in the correct way, included in the publication

- You should also be able to provide a note of when all birthdays are so that, if your piece isn't carried for ages (as can frequently happen) these can be updated

- Names, ages, occupations and address details of everyone else mentioned

Some of these may not end up being published, but you still need to know.

## KNOW YOUR AUDIENCE AND FOLLOW THE RELEVANT STYLE GUIDE

A busy, hard-pressed editor, with deadlines to meet, bosses to keep happy and a million admin tasks to see to, asks you to contribute a piece of writing because they feel it will be interesting, timely and worth reading. They expect you to write to their brief, so make sure you do so in a way that meets the style requirements of their publication. Study the newspaper or magazine carefully to learn what this means, or, in some cases, there may be a style guide. Stray from this at your peril.

## DON'T ASSUME ANYTHING

Never think that just because you know something your readers do too. Will they really be aware of the organisation you are referring to or know who your interviewee is? Even something as simple as spelling someone's name should be checked, however obvious you think it is. That leads us to...

## IS YOUR STORY TRUE? CHECK, CHECK AND CHECK AGAIN

Never assume anything you read elsewhere or are told is true. It's not just spelling that needs checking. Claims by PR people can be especially problematic. Who says that something is 'pioneering' or 'innovative' – what do they mean by a 'leading' company and how reliable are those 'survey' results?

News that a woman lauded as an inspirational survivor of the World Trade Center attacks was a fake sent a shiver down the spine. It was journalists' dogged detective work that revealed her lies, but how did she get to be so admired in the first place? I'd suggest there was a general feeling of why would anyone make this stuff up? As human beings, so many of us want to see the good in people.

But it should still be easy to check these stories out. As journalists, we have to go beyond the obvious and ask awkward questions that will reveal the truth, however uncomfortable that may be. You need to be cynical and often play devil's advocate.

With any story you are working on, you have to be able to stand it up, with the necessary checks and paper trail.

*This means you may have to:*

- Get copies of any birth, death or marriage certificates needed

- Speak to the police, council, court or other relevant authorities about details in the public domain

- Check with schools that people who claim they did really did go there

- Contact the local paper for any reports of court cases, inquests and so on that are either mentioned or you know will have resulted from your interviewee's claims

- Dig out, or convince people to hand over, relevant photos to show someone in a "past life"

- Speak to ex-partners, employers or estranged family, not only to check facts but also to give them 'right of reply'

- Investigate business records through Companies House

- Call on your in-built bullshit detector

## DON'T SAY TOO LITTLE

In my days as a news editor, I was fond of telling reporters that their copy 'begged too many questions'. The same frustration arises if you leave out information in your story that would help the reader better understand what you are reporting on.

Examples? Something basic would be saying that someone had won an award, but not what for and why. Or perhaps you are reporting on someone who has lost their job – help your reader by telling them what the job was, where it was, how much it paid and how long it had been held.

Another would be saying 'recently' when you need to be more specific or, in some circumstances, including a date and not saying what day of the week it is. You want the reader to know what you are talking about as quickly as possible. So if you tell them there's a meeting on January 19, why not also tell them this is a Monday to save them having to look it up? (I've heard this called 'news you can use', by the way, in case you like that sort of thing!).

Sounds obvious, doesn't it? Tell that to the next reporter who tells us about a 'miracle' baby born early and doesn't expand on how many weeks premature the child is, how much he or she weighed or how long they stayed in hospital.

Your story should answer all questions that a reader may ask as they go along, or that the subs may have about your copy.

An incidence of this would be:

You mention someone had to go to hospital:

- When did they go?

- Which hospital was it?

- What illness did they have?

- How long did they stay?

- Did anything happen in hospital that adds to the story?

Whatever the scenario, allow the story to develop naturally, including all the details needed to give the reader all they need to know. Sometimes this can be very involved and means you have to dig deep. You may have to ask difficult questions.

Your story should flow well, with no gaps of information to trip the reader up or leave them wondering what happened.

## SAYING TOO MUCH, TOO EARLY ON

You may be determined to include lots of important details in your copy. Please don't attempt to cram them all in to your introduction. Twenty words should be plenty. Remember, if someone has to read what you have written twice, then you have lost them and that's not good. Be economical with language and avoid cliché.

## BEING SUBJECTIVE RATHER THAN OBJECTIVE IN A NEWS STORY

You are reporting what's happening, not offering an opinion on it. A press release may tell you an achievement is 'impressive' or 'astounding' – but is it really? Who says? You should remain impartial at all times, offering sources with opposing views to express. You're not trying to show anyone how clever you are and analyse the information, as you may in a feature, you're reporting on it. There's a huge difference and again, as obvious as it sounds, journalists do overlook this. They can be too fond of their own voice. Include input from someone else analysing the facts presented instead, someone with relevant experience and authority.

## AVOID JARGON OR LANGUAGE THAT IS TOO COMPLICATED

Use as straightforward a language as possible. Your aim is to inform, not show how clever you are. Don't put your readers in mind of, say, a policeman reading evidence from a notebook. 'He was proceeding in a northerly direction' or some such nonsense. Don't say 'purchase' when you can say 'buy', don't say 'stationary', when you can say 'parked', for example. There are plenty more!

## USE LOTS OF DIRECT QUOTES

If you are going to report that someone has a view, back it up with direct quotes, else what's the point? Let your interviewees tell their story in their own words, where needed, to fit in with the word count available.

## DON'T WAFFLE ON

Be precise and succinct. Know when to stop.

## SUBS' QUERIES

If, after filing your copy, you need to be contacted to be asked lots of questions that haven't been answered, you won't exactly be presenting yourself in your best light.

Sometimes a sub may have a query you never saw coming, but, in hindsight, you can see why the information was needed.

Three that spring to mind for me:

- As a young reporter, I told the story of a woman who was robbed at gun point at a petrol station. I was feeling very pleased with myself to have convinced the victim to speak to me and to file my story within a tight timescale to make that day's paper. So when the phone call came from the news desk to tell me: 'You haven't said if she was buying diesel or petrol'. I wasn't best pleased. I'd hoped fuel was sufficient and, in the speed I'd had to prepare my copy (dictating it over the phone to a copy taster) from scribbles in my notebook, I'd overlooked to ask the question. Looking back now, it makes me smile – of course I should have found out!

- Writing an uplifting story about an injured woman for a high-selling weekly magazine and about how proud her sister was of her, I included some recollections about her wedding ceremony. I didn't describe what colour shoes she was wearing as I didn't think to ask. After a phone call from the magazine probing that very question, I was left in no doubt that this detail should have been included.

- In a regional Sunday tabloid, I wrote a story about a dad who left his family for another man. Questions followed about his sex life. I'd also asked them but hadn't included the answers as I felt this was "too much" information. The subs didn't agree.

You need to try and avoid being contacted by the subs to push you for more information. If they do contact you, you may be able to truthfully say you left out certain details because of the word count.

In my opinion, one of the worst things you can say when faced with a sub's query is: 'They didn't say'. Tell the truth. If you don't know, say so, but promise to find out as soon as you can and get back to them quickly. Don't moan or grumble about the extra work – you will be judged as much on how you react when faced with 'adds' needed as you will on your original copy. Keep your head up and remain professional. Get on with finding out what's needed.

## THIS COMES ABOVE WRITING STYLE

So long as it fits with house style and all questions are answered, you shouldn't stress over whether your copy ends up getting tinkered with by the subs. This isn't a writing competition, but a paid job where you have to meet the publication's requirements. Writing skill should be a given.

There are times when your writing will be changed and times you may be asked to rejig it yourself. When this happens, sort it out as quickly and as professionally as you can.

But if you miss an important fact because you haven't asked the right questions or found the right stuff out, then that's poor show.

If you are the writer an editor has to keep asking to make 'adds' they consider pretty basic then that will not be in your favour.

Based on my experience, I'd put the initial news gathering, research, interview technique – and getting all that's needed – above the importance of writing style.

## EVERY EDITOR IS DIFFERENT – BUT THEY ALL HAVE STANDARDS

In my personal life, I am quite happy-go-lucky but I know that, on a professional level, when new writers have approached me with their ideas or copy, for some reason they may have felt intimidated.

That's understandable when you are starting out. But I try to be respectful to writers and, when time and resources allow, communicate with and nurture contributors who deliver well and on time.

That said, there are also things that I don't want to have to put right. Putting them right twice gives me a headache.

Often, when I have worked on a new or developing publication, I have also compiled a style guide so writers can see at a glance what's expected of them.

Here are ten things that make me mutter far too much and wish people could put right before sending their work to me. In some publications, any of these, or a combination of them, could see your work dropped into the file marked: 'Don't darken our doorstep again' with no explanation or room for negotiation.

1. **Getting the name of the publication wrong**

   This really happens. You'd never do that, would you? Make sure you have the correct use of spacing, capitalisation and punctuation, don't just guess.

2. **Abusing the humble apostrophe**

   How difficult can it be to use an apostrophe correctly? Check out the Apostrophe Protection Society. If I'm going to allocate budget to your work, I need to see you know how to use such basic punctuation.

3. **Titles Or Headings Where You Insist On Making All The Words Have A Capital Letter... Plus, of course, Random Capital Letters Anywhere**

   Ouch. Sets my teeth on edge just thinking about it. Some publications may favour this approach, perhaps more so in the US, but try telling that to the poor reader who would like an easier experience, thanks.

4. **An addiction to exclamation marks!!!!!!**

   Now I have written that, I feel sick.

5. **Definately instead of definitely**

   Enough said.

6. **Alright instead of all right**

   Call me old-fashioned, call me a pedantic so and so, but I'm really not a fan of this new-fangled word. Apparently, it has been becoming more acceptable but if your copy is going to be used in a professional setting, it just may be best avoided.

7. **Underway instead of under way**

   Yes it's two words, in case you were wondering.

8.  **Numbers: Figures or words?**

    Do you say 10 or ten? One or 1? I know which I prefer, but check your
    target publication's style guide, if they have one. Or here's an idea,
    look at a copy or two and see how the other writers do it.

9.  **Over and out**

    Please don't say 'over' when you mean 'more than' and if you don't
    know the difference, find out.

10. **Using the wrong word**

    Refuted and electrocuted are my favourites I think, just because they
    come up so often. Again, if you don't know what I'm on about, check.

I know that some people reading this will disagree with some of these
points. That's fine, but when writing for any editor, bear in mind that they
may also have a list of 'cardinal sins' they don't want to see committed –
and definitely not repeated.

If you have your own blog, it's unlikely you have been employing a sub, so
learn all about grammar, syntax and media style and apply your new found
knowledge to make sure copy you submit as a paid job is as clean as it can be.

## ATTRIBUTION AND PLAGIARISM

At the time of going to press, the Independent columnist Johann Hari
was in the eye of a storm over alleged plagiarism. Fellow journalists
were publicly arguing over how serious it was that he appeared to have
'borrowed' large chunks of his work, with some claiming his reputation
was now in tatters. To avoid similar controversy, be clear on what you can
and can't include in what you write and how to make sure you credit all
sources where needed.

When a writer is accused of plagiarism, not only is their credibility affected,
but there's also a knock-on effect for others. No wonder journalists get a
bad name if high profile writers are 'busted' for shoddy work.

## AVOID ACCUSATIONS OF PLAGIARISM

- Gather your own information

- Carry out exclusive interviews

- Don't rely on the internet

- Give credit where credit is due and consider letting the other writer know you have done so

## PITCH YOUR HEART OUT

When should you pitch?

You have to time it right. And I don't mean pegging your suggested piece on a forthcoming awareness day, week or month. How many times have I read that awareness weeks make great hooks for stories? Yawn, that'll be too many. Beware. You can bet that if you know next month is bowel cancer awareness month, so will many other wannabe contributors. Again, what's so very new and different about your angle?

Lead-in times for publications vary. Pitch a monthly with a Christmas-type story in November and you are marking yourself out as someone who doesn't know what they are doing. Pick up the phone and find out when the deadlines for copy are.

How do you market your ideas then? It all comes down to your chosen market. Study your chosen publications or online markets carefully and make sure you send them what they ask for – to the right person at the right time.

## SHOULD YOU SEND YOUR PITCHES BY PHONE OR EMAIL?

I send most pitches by email. This gives the features or section editor time to digest it at their own pace. Some come back straight away. "Thanks for thinking of us, but it's not quite right. Good luck placing it elsewhere," says one editor, without fail, sometimes in the blink of an eye. How does she do that?

A colleague on another section of the newspaper says: "Thanks but I'll pass on this one." This usually takes him a day or so.

Some come back and say; "Yes please, X words ASAP" or words to that effect. I like it when a plan comes together!

And others never reply.

It's the editors in this last group who can cause the most anxiety for any freelancer.

That's why it pays not to leave it to chance. If you have real confidence in your idea, there's no harm in sending another email a little while later (say a week or two) asking for feedback, as politely as you can muster.

On one memorable day, I did this three times and clinched three commissions.

After that, you might like to phone. People seem to hate doing this. I used to be incredibly shy in all sorts of ways, so I can understand this, but if the choice is don't ring and not get the work or ring and find out the editor loves the idea but couldn't reply earlier due to covering for a colleague. Now which would you prefer? The £250 in the bank, I'd hope.

There is a time and place for everything, and sometimes even before, where instead of emailing, you've got to pick up that phone. And when might that be? Well, when the story's a cracker! That's when.

Examples? This is where the hugely-competitive but very financially rewarding human interest or so-called real life stories can come into their own.

Examples of stories I have placed include one about a woman who had triplets after a series of heart-breaking setbacks, another about a girl who was kept off school because bullies made her hair fall out, and a third about a woman who had a visit from the police over a missing shuttlecock.

My 'bravery', as some would have it, was rewarded with six immediate commissions, as I sold each story twice.

If you want to convince a magazine, newspaper or website editor they should commission a piece from you, you need to prove your idea:

- Would it fit well in their publication

- Is it worth writing **now**

- Would it be best written by you

- Will it be delivered well and on time

Miss out any of these elements and your pitch will fail.

This means you must include:

- A clear and compelling 'head' or title

- A great hook – what makes your contribution idea so timely?

- A succinct and compelling explanation of what your piece is about

- Information about you

Throughout your pitch, you must also show you're familiar with the usual content of the publication.

### BEFORE YOU PITCH

Study your target publication carefully. Does your idea really fit? Has it already been done? Would it really appeal to readers? Are you on the right wavelength? Can you see opportunities, or potential opportunities, for freelance contributions? If not, don't waste your time pitching! Check out any submission guidelines available online. The editor may have a blog explaining how to write for their section, or there may be a discussion on a writers' forum.

Be aware that many sections, which previously welcomed freelance contributions, may no longer do so due to budget constraints.

## LENGTH OF PITCH

Unless it's a really complicated area, the more compact the better – one paragraph is often plenty.

## 'ABOUT ME'

Include relevant information and links about your experience in the area you are aiming to write about in your target publication, plus any links to relevant articles already published, your professional website, or blog.

## WHERE AND WHEN TO SEND IT

Don't rely on outdated media lists or out of use online contacts. Find out the right person and send it direct to their email. If you can, find out when is the best time – depending on whether it's a daily, weekly or monthly publication.

You can start to find answers to these challenges by networking with other freelancers, enquiring with an editorial assistant or studying any guidelines provided.

## PITCHES THAT WORKED:

### Headhunted through Facebook – there's got to be a catch, right? (Telegraph)

*Social networking sites Facebook, Twitter and LinkedIn are becoming fertile ground for employers, as companies and recruiters head hunt for talent, and it's a trend that's reported to be on the increase – not to mention bloggers showcasing their skills to land plum jobs.*

*But what are the pitfalls for those doing the hiring and firing, and those seeking employment? Does this spell the end for the professional recruiter?*

### The Cha Cha Slide sent me into labour (Practical Parenting)

*We may have heard old wives' tales about curries, sex or possibly even walking up a hill starting labour – but what weird and wonderful happenings have helped some mums along the way? For some it was dancing to a favourite tune, for others it was the shock of a bill or an argument and for others, a hearty laugh at a favourite TV show (That was me!) I'd compile a feature on case studies with interesting experiences and offer advice from an expert on what to do when the crucial moment begins.*

So here's what you do. I've been asked for a template in the past so I hope this helps:

### PITCH TEMPLATE

In the subject field: Attention-grabbing title relevant to the publication you are pitching.

In the message: Hi (name of editor)

Re: Attention-grabbing title relevant to the publication you are pitching.

Then: One to three paragraphs explaining what you would like to write about. Be as succinct as possible. If you are suggesting more than one idea, then number them and space them out well.

Then: Thank you for your time, I'll welcome any feedback.

Then: A paragraph headed 'About me'. Explain why you are the right person to write this piece, listing relevant experience and links to any published work.

Don't forget to include all contact details – home, work, mobile, the lot. You won't be very popular if they can't get hold of you to commission your long-laboured-over gem of an idea.

## MAKE YOUR HEADING WORK FOR YOU

What do I mean by attention-grabbing?

Here are three of my headings that worked:

Mummy, that lady has a beard! (Take a Break)

My Boxing Day hangover was triplets (Pick Me Up)

My daughters' school reports are complete drivel (Independent)

And here are three that didn't:

Diary of a Virtual Assistant (Boring!)

Can marriages be saved by counselling? (What was I thinking?)

From midwife to ghosthunter (Hmm, quite liked that one!)

## THE 'SO WHAT?' TEST

Think about what is so different about your idea. Why is it current now? And why are you the one to write it? A general piece on 'home education' might not be deemed worth looking at, and could easily be researched and written in-house. But a piece on home education with a cracking interview with a mum who refuses to send her son to school because of bullies, might be nearer the mark – especially if there has been a topical or newsworthy development on a national scale.

## NOT MANY CUTTINGS SO FAR? DON'T DESPAIR!

Your life experience might be much more attractive to an editor than a clutch of cuttings from someone without your passion. Just don't let that passion run away with you in your pitch.

A lawyer might be considered to be in a better position to pitch an article about a miscarriage of justice than a more dispassionate and established writer, so long as their pitch is well presented, concise, and engaging. It all depends on the style of the article and how expert the writer is. In this particular example, some editors might question partiality, but, most often, 'insider knowledge' can be a definite plus.

## FOLLOWING UP

So you haven't had a response to your lovingly crafted, concise pitch with a hook to die for? Don't panic.

Editors are human too.

Perhaps they are away from their desk, perhaps they are working on a special project or standing in for a colleague.

Maybe they picked up your pitch, thought ''hmm this looks interesting'' but haven't had time to come back to you.

Just possibly, they no longer have money allocated for freelance contributions and, in the million things they have to do, replying to you isn't top of the list.

They may not even have seen your pitch in the sea of emails they receive in any given day. What they are likely not doing, if your pitch is well put together, is thinking: 'What a load of rubbish, I really must put a black mark against this chancer and resolve never to enter into correspondence with them!'

Whatever you do, don't assume the worst. You can follow up effectively. Depending on the lead-in times or newsworthiness of your hook, you may want an answer quickly, or you can follow up at a later date without wanting to look too ''pushy.''

If you need a quick answer, then pick up the phone at an appropriate time, depending on what the publication is.

If it's a monthly publication, for example, there's no harm in sending a polite email a week or so later, with 'Seeking feedback on pitch' – with your original attention-grabbing headline in the subject field.

Still no answer? Then leave it another week and phone. Make sure you phone at a convenient time – not when a section editor, for example, is likely to be tied up with the finishing touches to that week's edition.

If you don"t know what day this is – find out. This really does work.

Plan what you want to say before picking up the phone and aim to sound as upbeat as possible. You may get a "no" – but this can be for all sorts of reasons – perhaps they already have a piece planned on a similar theme, perhaps space has been cut back because of a special feature or more advertising.

Once, when I pitched an education section, when I followed up on the phone, I got a 'nice idea but already been planned in, in another article.' I immediately sent the pitch to another editor who said 'yes please and can I have it by 11am, please do it this way...'

Even the most experienced freelancers can hear "no" more than they hear "yes" – but if your ideas are good enough, are targeted at the right editors at the right time, then you are likely to break through at some point. But it is getting harder.

It's easier said than done, but if you are determined, stay positive – and polish your pitches to give them the best chance possible – in the meantime.

## CAN YOU SEND THE SAME PITCH TO DIFFERENT EDITORS?

Yes you *can* – but it's not always a good idea. It depends on the individual pitch and target publication.

Obviously, if your idea is expertly crafted to meet the needs of a specific slot, then it'd be pretty ridiculous to send it elsewhere without changing it.

Or if you are gagging to break a new market, then you may want to concentrate on that first before going down a list of the best editors to send it to, one by one.

But you don't *always* have to wait for the first one to come back before you offer it elsewhere.

Some editors can get terribly annoyed by this, but if you know your markets, you'll know when this is the case – and when it is a suitable plan. Like lots of things in freelance journalism, a feel for when this is the right thing to do comes with experience.

It depends on how timely the piece is and how strong a story it is.

Pitching to women's magazines, for example, can result in editors coming back with a yes or no very quickly.

Of course, if you do send it to various editors, there's even a chance of more than one editor wanting it. There's nothing wrong with saying that you have sold it elsewhere – it can be good to be in demand. However, this is a risky strategy and you may end up annoying an editor. So think carefully.

If you have a news story you don't think can wait, then pick up that phone, tell the news desk and follow instructions – they might want you to follow up on it, or they might ask a staff writer to take the details. Either way, you can pocket a cheque and, for the time it's taken to make a phone call, that can be more than worth your while, so long as you don't put the phone down without settling on your fee.

Your local paper might not have the budget to reward you handsomely, but what about the nationals? Read the tabloids – what sort of news stories are they featuring and could you supply them? Personally, I wouldn't get into the 'kiss and tell' shenanigans – but what about the quirky, off-the-wall stories that raise a smile? They all have to come from someone. Why shouldn't it be you? Keep your ear to the ground in your local community and who knows what you might discover.

## HIT THAT TARGET

When pitching features, you could have the best idea in the world, but if it's sent to the wrong place, it will stand what's technically known as a snowball-in-hell's chance.

Get to know the sections you want to take a shot at. Are their pages filled with by-lines from staffers or are they open to freelancers? What regular slots are there and are they on a theme or in a style you are confident you could match?

How do you know if you'll hit the spot? Research, research, and research again. Start small, with 'fillers' and letters – they can pay a small amount and shouldn't take up too much time.

## WHERE TO SEND YOUR PITCH?

I've browsed many a website looking for 'contacts' at different publications – what a waste of time that was! Despite the advice from the "amateur scribes" online (their words, not mine!), who give a postal address and tell you to send a hard copy in a brown envelope, written out in pen, your best bet is to get the exact name and direct phone number and email address of the section editor you are targeting.

## HOW DO YOU DO THAT THEN?

Well, you could ring the paper or magazine. Yes really. If this scares the pants off you, listen very carefully, I shall say this only once: you might not be cut out for freelancing. It involves, like, talking to people. Or (even more shocking) you could buy the publication and look for any list of staff included to select your prey, sorry, contact. There might also be an editorial assistant that you could contact but beware, this might be the busiest person on the features desk, so don't always expect a warm welcome.

## KEEPING YOUR CARDS CLOSE TO YOUR CHEST

Some freelance journalists choose not to name the people they want to write about in their pitches to editors, or even change their names. They do this because they have had their fingers burned and can tell you about instances when their idea or case study was passed on to someone on an in-house editorial team. I think this is a terrible shame and would hate that to happen. I've not encountered it. I tend to give as many details as I can to help make the decision to commission me as easy as possible – but, at the same time, I do my utmost to show why I am in a unique position of being able to interview the people involved or write the story myself. Perhaps it's luck that I haven't been ripped off in this way. Keep your wits about you but don't be too cloak and dagger.

## BUT ISN'T PHONE BETTER THAN EMAIL?

Again, it depends. Editors are so busy now that they won't take kindly to you ringing right on deadline to pitch an idea, however good it is. Nor will they welcome a zillionth email, chasing them over an idea you first sent just three days ago.

So what can you do? Finding out when they are least likely to be busy, for a start. Yes, it's their job to look at freelance pitches (possibly) but please don't moan if they don't reply. I've said it before and I'll say it again – they didn't ask you to contact them, so why should they race to reply?

## AFTER THE COMMISSION

Send your copy on time. Keep your editor informed of any potential obstacles to meeting your deadline, if they are serious enough, but otherwise get on with it. Once you have filed, don't expect any reply. It's great to get feedback that says; "Lovely copy, thanks" but editors' workloads aren't going to let that happen all the time. Don't worry, no news is good news.

## WRITING ON SPEC

There are exceptions to every rule. Some publications might welcome on spec, unsolicited, fully researched and written articles, so please do not write to me to tell me that Leek Growers' Weekly once published your fascinating article about pest control.

But by far the best idea, when targeting any publication, is to get in touch with an idea that gains the editor's interest, allowing them to advise you how many words they want and in which direction they would like you to take it. Forget labouring over a 1,000 article to send off to a new editor. What's the point of that? They might love the idea but want you to take it in a wholly different direction. And they're the boss.

If you have already sweated over a completed piece, you may have wasted your time.

Having said that, if you do contact some more esteemed publications (The Sunday Times springs to mind) then, as a new writer, you might be asked to write your piece on spec, to see if you meet the required standard. What do you do then? Some people waver but my advice is go for it.

What can I expect from pitching?

Aspiring freelance journalists have often asked me what a 'typical' hit rate is for pitches. It's one of those 'how long is a piece of string?' questions and the answer depends on factors such as:

- Who you were pitching

- The ideas you sent

- What your specialism is

- If you know the editor…

- Plus, I'm sure, many more

I thought it may be useful to recount how I got on recently when I pretty much spent a day pitching. I sent nine ideas, contacting five editors. Some ideas were included in more than one pitch, adapted to target the different publications.

*This resulted in:*

One 'thanks you are on the right lines so keep trying as we have done something a bit similar.' This was a broadsheet newspaper's specialist online section, in response to one idea.

One 'first two could work, will discuss them in a meeting in a few weeks time'. That was the response of an editor on a monthly magazine for families, for whom I'd already written three features.

One, 'not for us, thanks' – which was another section of a broadsheet, in the paper as opposed to online. I really would love to crack that one – I've tried about three times now and have sparked interest in the past – but no firm commissions.

One complete silence from a health magazine.

One 'yes please 1,400 words by next Wednesday'. This was from an editor on a tabloid newspaper I have pitched twice before, with my last idea falling at the hurdle of a features conference.

Each of these responses took a week or so to reach me, and most came after a prompt from a second, really polite email from me.

I hadn't pitched for ages so was feeling a bit uneasy. I'm pleased that there was a fair return on a day's time spent pitching.

### HOW MANY IDEAS SHOULD YOU SEND IN A PITCH?

How many have you got? It's totally up to you – anywhere between one and 10 may be suitable for the editors I've contacted, depending on the publication, how often it comes out, how new it is (if you are trying to get hold of a regular gig, then more ideas may be a sound approach) but it's quality not quantity that matters. In my experience, sending three or five ideas at a time to a features editor can work well. But one strong news suggestion can also have the desired effect. Get to know your editors and understand how they work, then you will have a far better idea of what they would like to be presented with – and just how ridiculous they may find the prospect of you flooding their inbox with 10 ideas in one go.

## DEALING WITH REJECTION

How scared are you of editors? Does the thought of picking up a phone to suggest an idea for a magazine feature fill you with dread? Do you break out in a cold sweat as you open an email with the all-important "yes" or "no" to your pitch?

If you're nodding in agreement to either of these questions, then, to put it unkindly, you need to get a grip! Or, to put it much less bluntly – don't worry, editors are human too.

But to see the correspondence I receive seeking advice from aspiring or, in some cases, established freelance writers, you'd think these more senior journalists were ogres – who'd chew up and spit out humble wannabe hacks without a moment's thought.

I find this frustrating.

So long as you are professional in your dealings with your chosen editors, you have nothing to worry about. Sure, they may say 'no' to more of your ideas than 'yes' – but that's nothing to lose sleep over is it? Don't take rejection personally. Look at what, if anything, you could have done differently and keep going.

There are lots of reasons why an editor may not have the time to get back to you – and none of them is a comment on the quality of your work.

And always remember that, like all of us, editors can make mistakes too – they may even do that in connection with stuff you are working on for them.

One writer once told me that she'd always considered editors to be "God-like and infallible" – but then one made some mistakes with her piece, which absolutely convinced her that this wasn't the case!

Journalism lecturer and feature writer Carrie Dunn told me, during feature research, that being scared of editors can be a "fundamental" part of being a writer.

She says: "It's the power thing. Editors hold the power of yes and no over us, so fundamentally it's down to them whether we get paid or not. Some editors cultivate distance and revel in seeming a bit scary! There are one or two I'm slightly intimidated by, but I like all my regular editors.

"It took me a while to get round the fact that editors are nice people too.

"The best way to build respect from an editor is to give them the material they want in a professional, clean and precise fashion.

"They're not always going to like you as a person and you're not always going to be friends with them, but that doesn't stop them from thinking you're a good journalist!"

Also, don't forget that some editors are in the same boat as you. They may also work as freelance writers.

And there's a strong possibility that, even if they are no longer in a position of trying to convince a different editor their ideas are worth reporting on, they may well have previously been there. Carrie adds: "I'd say a good proportion of editors are also freelancers – people just like you are the ones commissioning. Think of it like that and they'll soon seem less intimidating."

Rachel Newcombe is a respected journalist and editor with a pragmatic view. She says: "I don't think it's much help to a writer to be scared of editors, since the large majority of their work will involve pitching to and working with them.

"Admittedly, it can be a bit scary to approach an unknown editor for the first time, but if you want to pitch for work or have a chance of writing for their magazine or newspaper, then you have to get over your nerves and get stuck into it."

And Rachel says that, in order to banish that somewhat irrational fear, writers should "remember that editors are only human too." She agrees with Carrie: "Plus, although they're in a position of authority now, the chances are they started out on the same rung of the ladder as a writer, so they do have some knowledge of what it's like to be pitching people."

Rachel, who previously edited Health Today magazine and Buying Abroad, a property magazine distributed with the Telegraph and Sunday Telegraph, also underlines that there is no sense in taking rejection personally.

"Pitches are rejected for a whole host of reasons, such as not being quite right for the slot, a similar topic is already being covered or that something similar has been featured recently.

"Sometimes it is the case that the writer hasn't quite grasped the essence of the publication, that they're pitching the wrong type of idea to the magazine or don't have quite the right experience (yet), but getting rejections is all part of the learning curve," she says. "Rather than taking it personally, the best thing a writer can do is learn from their rejections."

There will probably be many times when pitches come back with a short and sharp 'no' and no other further explanation, but, on other occasions, some editors take the time to explain why it's not right. You can learn lots from reading through the more detailed responses and taking the details in. If all you get back is a 'no' though, you can still learn by reading the publication thoroughly and studying the type of articles that they tend to use.

It's also good to talk to other writers and see if those currently writing for the publications can offer any extra insight into the type of pitches typically accepted.

It's good to work at crafting better pitches to editors.

Sarah Drew-Jones has been a journalist and editor for around 20 years and her credits include The Guardian, the BBC and the Sunday Mirror.

As a former head of magazines at Trinity Mirror, she has had plenty of experience of being pitched – well and not so well – by aspiring freelance writers. She says that it's obvious that, in these days of growing pressure on editors, they simply may not have the time to build a relationship with you.

"No, writers shouldn't be scared of editors, but they should try to be respectful in their dealings with them, as well as, of course, be friendly, professional and efficient," advises Sarah.

"The best editors will understand (and remember) what it's like to be a young writer, but these days they are so busy and under so much pressure that their ability to advise, chat, give feedback or even build any kind of relationship with you is severely limited."

So how do you keep on the right side of an editor? Sarah has some straight-talking advice. "The best thing any new or young writer can do is be ruthlessly efficient. Pitch short, succinct, well-explained ideas, meet (or try to beat) any deadline given, go the extra mile when possible (for example, supply pictures or sidebars) and ensure your copy is immaculate."

"This is the best way to get editors to not only like you, but rate you and remember you, too."

She also has some excellent pointers on learning how not to take rejection personally.

"A mentor once advised me to think of myself in the same way that an actor does. A pitch is like an audition – sometimes you're not 'wrong' you're just not right for that part. Journalists need thick skins, and taking rejection personally is a motivation killer."

Dust yourself down, take your idea somewhere else and keep new ones flowing: some of them will work! The only thing you should take personally is constructive criticism.

If an editor gets back to you to say they loved your original idea but you didn't execute it well when you filed your copy, that's when you know you've got a problem.

Ask for feedback and work on it, whether it's grammatical sloppiness or a lack of research. Everyone can improve and the sense of achievement it'll give you when your next piece is accepted will be immense.

## NEGOTIATING RATES

When will an editor ask you what your rates are?

In my experience, an editor is most likely to ask you this if:

1. They are advertising for a writer or writers and in the ad they stipulate that you should state your rates. This may be a new or established market for freelance writers or journalists.

2. Theirs is a new publication recruiting freelance writers and they either advertise or you hear on the grapevine that they need contributors.

3. Theirs is an established market and they want you to write a series of articles or ask you to submit ideas and rates.

## WHEN WON'T IT HAPPEN?

- In my experience, it doesn't happen so often with more high-profile markets. These should have clearly set fees for their freelance contributors.

- There are established freelance rates, which may be discussed by freelance writers, debated on forums or listed in the NUJ Rate for the Job guide.

- Not all publications will pay these rates. Clear advice from the NUJ is that these rates should be viewed as minimum rates when writing for the media listed in their guide.

When your pitch is accepted by a national newspaper or magazine, for example, the editor should confirm a rate with you. More experienced contributors may request more money depending on the task.

## WHAT TO SAY WHEN IT DOES

It depends on which of the three situations above applies.

With situations one and two, I'd explain that I work for a number of publications paying different rates, some much higher than others. If pushed for a figure, I say that I work for publications that pay between the lowest fee I am happy to accept and one that's higher.

If I know that many more writers will be applying, I currently say that my preferred minimum rates are those advised by the NUJ, of around £350 per thousand words.

But regardless of which situation applies, the preferred option will always be: Ask what the budget is.

## TAKE THE OPPORTUNITY TO CLARIFY THE BRIEF

I will politely ask questions about how much work is needed and when it's needed by.

If the new editor's reply suggests they are testing the water, alarm bells ring and I steer clear.

If they have started out and their business model or plan hasn't factored in paying the writer a decent fee, then it's a commonly held view that it must stink.

Companies should always have a budget in mind, so they must be being run pretty shoddily if they haven't got one – whether they want to tell you or not is another matter.

It may be that they have set their budget for freelance writers lower than you are prepared to work for. Establishing what it is can save you the time, effort and stress of going any further. Suggested rates can be shockingly low – so the sooner you know what they are the better.

Once I have this information, I am much more likely to know whether I want to continue.

I feel confident setting my rate at the level I do because I've done my homework and will have researched the potential work and the going rate. I don't apply if I think rates will be too low.

## WHEN WOULD I WORK FOR A LOWER RATE?

I have worked for lower rates but there have been reasons behind this:

- I know they are prompt payers. Sometimes a lower fee paid quickly can have a positive impact on cash flow

- I know I can re-jig and resell the work or use the research to land higher paying commissions

- I consider the job a definite stepping stone to a higher paid job

- I'm keen to raise awareness with my article (for example, writing for a charity's magazine with a limited budget)

- That the job will help me develop new skills that I can make use of for a greater profit (for example, writing for a commercial blogging company)

- The work can be done very quickly and when you take into account the time it will take me and how straightforward it is, I consider it will provide a good return on my investment of time

- It will boost my career in other ways

## BECAUSE YOU'RE WORTH IT

In my commercial writing workshops, I advise that, when working with clients outside of journalism, if you compete on price you may lose a job on price.

This means you should do your best to show a potential customer why your service is excellent regardless of your price and whether or not it's higher than that of another supplier.

I'd suggest this may be easier to do outside of journalism – where there aren't so many aspiring writers willing to undercut you, or budgets may be more flexible, even now.

But the basic principle of being able to explain why you are worth paying a decent rate still holds true.

You should still aim to convince editors that your rate is worth paying and do all you can to explain it.

*When negotiating rates, you should always aim to:*

- Set out your experience

- Include details of similar work undertaken

- Provide evidence of specialist knowledge

- Give details of a testimonial or reference from a previous job

So you are showing them more about why you are right for the job than stressing your rate.

When you state your rate, you should have always:

- Considered how long the job will take you

- Thought about how much effort it will take – do you need to find case studies, for example, and interview them, or is the research more straightforward?

- Factored in any expenses or clarified if expenses can be charged separately

- If you decide to turn the rate down – do so politely and professionally. There is no reason why you shouldn't.

## BUILDING A SPECIALISM

Starting out as a freelance journalist can be a nail-biting time, as pitch after pitch is rejected or, worse, ignored.

But if you can carve out a reputation as a specialist in a certain area, you can put yourself ahead of some of the competition.

By impressing editors with your knowledge of a niche subject, you can ensure they come knocking when the time is right. That means you could find yourself in demand when a new publication launches or when your expertise is timely, thanks to a big news story.

Sign up to research documents, specialist publications and even foreign journals relating to your chosen field. Get to know of, and keep in touch with, experts in the same field, keep track of new developments and innovations and show editors how on-the-ball you are. Keep a blog, detailing latest news in the subject area, seeking and responding to comments from other interested parties. Attend conferences, meetings or trade shows.

But, warns health writer Rachel Newcombe, you should choose your specialism carefully.

"If it's too much of a niche subject, it could narrow your chances of work. But if you choose a popular topic, you'll be up against more experienced journalists who are likely to have the contacts and get the most lucrative work. Find the right balance."

For some journalists, their specialism is a natural extension of a previous career.

Former teacher Janet Murray says: "I had my first piece in the Times Educational Supplement when I was still on my journalism training course: a first-person piece about why I'd left teaching!"

Building and looking after the right contacts is key. Join professional associations, subscribe to relevant journals and keep an eye out for news from across the world – could a piece in a US or Australian publication spark a similar feature closer to home?

"As I began to establish contacts – from teachers themselves to education PRs and professional bodies – I found I was inundated with story ideas, so I could pitch more education editors," says Janet.

Being known as a specialist has been a massive boost to her freelance career, she adds. "Once you're established, 'cold pitching' becomes rare. If you concentrate on building relationships with the editors in your specialist area, often they'll come to you with commissions as well as giving all your ideas serious consideration."

A web presence is also vital. "Having developed your specialism, it's important to ensure that others are aware of it and that you become known as an expert. Having a website is invaluable," says Rachel. Maintaining a blog on your niche subject can also add to your standing in the field.

Rachel adds that sometimes your specialism can end up surprising you.

"Don't rule out having more than one focus. Sometimes there may be a topic that links well with your main subject and could broaden possibilities for you," she says.

"But you can also try a secondary subject in a completely different area. I've ended up specialising in foreign property, too, which is a complete contrast to health but just as interesting in its own way."

### IDEAS ARE EVERYWHERE

You can, if you choose, turn every experience you encounter in your life – or find out about other people's – into the potential inspiration for a feature. From family activities to your views on reality TV, there is a possible market to be found. Take your notepad everywhere – ideas can crop up in the strangest of places.

Read your favoured publications regularly. What topics are they covering and how could you contribute?

Sign up to news alerts from Google, read the BBC online, check out sites that distribute press releases relating to the subjects that you are interested in. These are all fine examples of ways to keep up-to-date with what's happening in the world, or certain parts of it. But also, don't forget about people. Find interesting characters in your chosen field with intriguing or inspirational tales to tell and help them with their stories. Study all the specialist or weekly magazines you can to realistically predict where your pitch could find a home.

Let talking to people be the backbone of your research. An enthusiastic, charismatic or inspirational human being will help you with food for thought far more than any printed document, in my opinion.

## ALREADY BEEN DONE?

So you want to write for your favourite magazine and you are brimming with ideas – you're a little disappointed that most of them – or something similar at least – has been covered already – but it's still worth a shot, right?

Wrong. If you spot a piece in a target publication that bears any resemblance to the germ of an idea you have been slaving over – but are too nervous to send – for days or even weeks then you need to change direction immediately. First pause a moment to congratulate yourself that you are on the right wavelength – then move on, pronto!

Either come up with a new angle to suit a different sort of market, or start again.

You have to find something that is different, new and fresh, but, at the same time, relevant and newsworthy.

## WHEN EDITORS ASK FOR MORE

As a freelance journalist, it's inevitable that now and again editors will ask you for more work on a piece – once you have already filed. It's a situation that can make your heart sink – but can often be met with good humour – or avoided in the first place.

Freelance travel, health and fashion journalist Lucia Cockroft says it happens in around 5 to 10 per cent of features. "In some cases, the original brief is vague. This can be rectified if the writer goes back to the editor for clarification immediately," she says. "Sometimes it's a case of the editor just wanting additional information."

Lucia adds that, despite the extra demands on her time, she doesn't consider it the right approach to ask for an increased fee if the editor's demands are reasonable.

"If the editor was making unfair demands, such as asking for additional interviews that would take a significant amount of time, I would ask for more money," she says. "In most cases, however, I just accept that sometimes more work is needed."

We've all been there. Accepting "adds" may be needed and getting on with them is part of the job.

If you're going to insist on your rights every five minutes, then you won't find much work or editors to put up with you.

But there is a point where you may consider your editor is being unreasonable. Tread carefully. Perhaps let them know that the 11th set of adds you are being asked to do didn't fit with the original brief. You have to find a balance between not being a doormat and, as Kelly Rose Bradford told us in chapter two, trying very hard not to annoy people.

Christine Michael has edited six magazines and now oversees the Diabetes Choices website. She stresses that communication and flexibility are at the heart of a strong working relationship and can avoid problems.

She says: "It's quite rare that I've asked a writer to redo a piece completely. I've generally preferred to work on a brief with a writer in order to be confident the copy is going to be pretty much as I expect it to be.

"For an editor, having a detailed house style guide that covers policy issues can save a lot of time and misunderstandings."

"Sometimes you do have to change the goalposts – for example, the submitted piece may have ended up too similar to something that's appeared recently, or you may find something in it that takes the feature in a more interesting, unexpected direction," she says.

"I like writers to let me know if this happens as they're working on a piece, so we can agree how to take it forward.

"It's great to find writers who are willing to be flexible and keen to get the piece right.

"I'm much more likely to re-commission writers I can build a good relationship with."

## OKAY, SO EDITORS MAY MOVE THE GOALPOSTS, CAN YOU?

No. Don't do anything outside of your brief unless you have checked it with your editor first.

Perhaps, due to time pressures, people you needed to speak to aren't available, or change their mind about speaking to you. Maybe someone doesn't want to cooperate with you any more, which can seriously affect your story. Believe it or not, I've known instances where I have been working as an editor and a contributor has filed copy with holes such as these, without mentioning anything was amiss.

That isn't an ideal situation for an editor or writer to find themselves in.

Sometimes you may feel, after carrying out some of your research, or talking to people involved in your commission, that, actually, you now have a better story than the one you were asked to work on.

Don't get carried away. Your editor may or may not agree with you. Talk to them about it and see what they think. Listen to their guidance, don't assume you are on the right track.

In short, don't stray from your brief without consulting your editor first. And if things go wrong, tell them. We are all human, some things will be out of your control. Don't ignore it, hoping the problem will go away, and file incomplete or unexpected copy. Do so and you could be in big trouble.

## CHECKLIST: MAGAZINE ARTICLE

Tick off all of the following to make sure your magazine article will hit the mark:

Who: Get the basics right. Have you checked how to spell everyone's names? Be sure to put "all names correct" in a note at the end of your copy. Do you understand their relationship to everyone else in the piece?

Find out: Age; address; job; contact details, relationship with other people and birthday (will they be another year older by the time the piece comes out?).

Learn about the right to reply and where it's needed. Find relevant expert comments if it's needed: use a bona fide expert – not just someone attempting to publicise their own work.

What: Do you understand exactly what has happened, or is going to happen, and why? Can you explain this clearly and succinctly? Remember there's no such thing as a stupid question. If they have to read any part of it twice, then you've failed.

When: Know your lead-in times. It's no good pitching a Christmas article in November or a Valentine's piece in February. Monthly magazines plan for months ahead and even weekly magazines can have a long wait.

Look at the way your story pans out – if you are telling a personal story, then start at the beginning and tell it chronologically, rather than using an intro that attempts to pack in all the facts.

Check all your dates are correct before you submit: Often the style of the publication may be to include the day of the week, the date and the month.

Know what's happening with pictures: Is the magazine taking their own? Do they need "collects" (Family album pictures or those submitted by an interviewee)?

Tell the story: Include as much detail and colour as you can, without waffling on. Use short sentences that help the reader along. Introduce dialogue where necessary and keep the flow.

Where: They may not care as much as a paper, but it's important to get locations right. Sometimes even the sub editors might get it wrong, so give them all the help you can by getting it right in the first place.

How's your intro? Hook the reader in.

Spell check again and again: Just in case you've inadvertently changed some words to something quite different. It can happen, you know, and when it does, it might be hilarious, but the telling off you get if the first time it's spotted is in the magazine, won't be.

Above all: Meet requirements. Follow your brief to the letter – word count and deadline haven't been put there for fun. Get them wrong and there may not be a next time.

## CHECKLIST: NEWSPAPER ARTICLE

Tick off all of the following to make sure your newspaper article cuts the mustard:

Who: Have you checked how to spell everyone's names? Be sure to put "all names correct" in a note at the end of your copy.

Find out: Age; address; job; contact details, relationship with other people and birthday (will they be another year older by the time the piece comes out?). Make sure the people interviewed are relevant to the readership of the publication.

What: Do you understand exactly what has happened, or is going to happen, and why? Can you explain this clearly and succinctly? Remember there's no such thing as a stupid question. If they have to read any part of it twice, then you've failed.

When: Check all your dates are correct before you submit. Often the style of the publication may be to include the day of the week, the date and the month.

Why and how: Often the best part of the story! Answer any questions that arise – half the story is no good. Put yourself in the readers' position again and ask away!

Where: A local paper might want a street name, but not a more widely read publication.

Use the right style: Check out current or past editions of the publication you're writing for to make sure you are on the right track.

Mind your language: Don't use six words to say something you could in one. Avoid jargon and just keep it simple.

A capital offence: Legalese may demand every second word be capped up, but not a newspaper.

A question of spelling and grammar: One "definately" is one too many. The same goes for womens, banana's or 1970's.

How's your intro? Any more than 30 words and it could be a no-no. Make your readers read on.

Limit sentences per paragraph: Three might be too many.

Let your fingers do the talking: Make your copy come alive: use a mix of direct and indirect speech. Quotes should be exciting, interesting and thought-provoking. Don't get carried away with the exclamation marks or descriptive verbs.

Spell check again and again: Just in case you've inadvertently changed some words to something quite different. It might be hilarious, but the telling off you get if the first time it's spotted is in the paper, won't be.

Play fair: Unless it's an opinion piece, make sure you have given any opposing viewpoints a balanced, unbiased slice of the action. And even if it is an opinion piece, still play fair! Make sure nothing you have written is offensive or potentially libellous. If you're not sure what this means, you're not ready to start.

Above all: Meet requirements. Follow your brief to the letter – word count and deadline haven't been put there for fun. Get them wrong and there may not be a next time.

# Popular Pursuits: Real Life Stories and Travel Writing

*" If you want to get rich from writing, write the sort of thing that's read by persons who move their lips when they're reading to themselves. "*

Don Marquis

# Chapter 5

# Popular Pursuits: Real Life Stories and Travel Writing

## KERCHING! REAL LIFE STORIES

Did you know a top notch story in a women's weekly magazine or tabloid 'real life' section could bring you thousands of pounds? Perhaps you did – and maybe you fancy a piece of the action.

But beware. As well as being one of the most lucrative areas of freelance journalism, unsurprisingly, because of the high stakes, it's also one of the most daunting and competitive – and not one to be entered into lightly.

These publications include inspirational and heartwarming tales about everyday people who have battled through adversity. But, of course, they also feature hard-hitting stories peppered with tragedy, crime, sex or violence.

Your job is to find them and make them compelling... and it's easier said than done.

When I wrote about this highly competitive area of journalism, magazine writer Sally Wilson told me: "You have to be self-motivated – for every one 'yes' to a commission, there are about seven 'nos' to other pitches.

"I do real life exclusively and though the money's good – I almost tripled my salary from my staff job as a writer at a weekly magazine – it's positively soul-destroying when, after days and days of searching, chatting to your prospective interviewee and organising photos, the magazine decides it doesn't have enough 'whizzes and bangs' – even though it's a cracking story in its own right."

Fellow freelance and senior magazine journalist Judy Yorke agreed.

She says: "You need a few rather conflicting qualities to succeed in the real life market.

"First, you need to be able to spot a story and work up a great coverline. Second, you need to be ruthless enough to secure the story ahead of anyone else chasing it. Third, you need to be a fairly sympathetic person (or a good actress!) because many of these are sad stories. If you're a nasty, ruthless person, you won't be able to sympathise with the person you're talking to and make them feel comfortable."

My own advice is that, if the thought of having to quiz someone on a wayward partner's fling with the vicar fills you with dread, or you're appalled at the "tawdriness" of it, leave it alone. You won't be any good at it.

Asking the 'right' questions is key. It's not enough to know how old someone is, how many children they have, or what their husband does for a living. You have to be creative, find a quirky 'line' with an emotional 'pull' – one that can draw readers in as a potential coverline – that succinct sentence on the front of the magazine that makes you want to read the story inside.

Sally, who has written for titles including Take a Break, Love it!, Bella, Best, Pick Me Up and Chat, as well as the Mirror, Express, Mail and Sun, says: "I write letters to people on the back of stories I've seen in newspapers. Sometimes, it's a stab in the dark – and I'm hoping to find an extra line to the story than the one that's been in the newspaper. I need to ask the 'right' questions to secure those gem-encrusted lines. Sadly, it doesn't always work but, when it does, it's fantastic."

Many slots in women's magazines pay around £500 to £1,000. You have to dig deep to find these stories. If they've been anywhere else, forget it. The magazines want exclusives.

Building contacts is also key – earn their trust and look after them.

The gift of the gab goes a long way – if you can't charm the birds out of the trees, you've got to at least keep trying.

This is even more important as the market shrinks and the competition becomes more fierce.

Judy explains: "Stories have become much more sensational and much more celebrity-led. When I was first commissioning at Woman, about 10 years ago, it was all miracle babies and children with rare syndromes. Those stories are very hard to place now. Editors much prefer I was £50,000 in debt because I wanted to look like Jordan or sex slave stories."

Sally adds: "Editors are asking for ludicrous scenarios. The amount of times I've heard something to the effect of…"I'd have taken the story if the guy had been wearing red underpants, not blue ones. It's really frustrating.

"Everything needs to be backed up by good photographs, too. You might have a diamond story but, unless there's a picture of each key element of the story, it won't work."

So, once you have what you hope is the best tale since your neighbour plunged £50,000 into debt trying to look like Jordan, how do you persuade an editor to agree with you?

It's all in the pitch.

Judy, who has been assistant features editor at Good Housekeeping and spent five years as features editor at Woman, before going freelance, advises: "If you have a good story, read all the magazines in the market. Decide who best to pitch it to, think of a great coverline, write a short pithy paragraph and send it to the commissioning editor on your chosen magazine.

"Tell them a picture is available but don't send it unless asked, because you will clog up their inbox. If you don't hear back, follow up the next day and move on to the next magazine.

"And you have to be honest – don't lie about where else the story has been – if you do, you will be found out and you won't be paid."

You also have to show you know what you are doing. Can you get all the documentation needed? Have you "stood up" the story with the right authorities and sought comment from any other party? No? Better get it sorted.

And then we're on to the writing. Put yourself in your readers' shoes. Give them a cracking read.

While we are on the subject of the actual writing, Judy sounds a note of caution.

She says: "The magazines don't really care who is selling the story – they routinely re-interview case histories anyway. So if your copy is rubbish, they'll just throw it in the bin and start again. Sadly, the quality of the writing is just about the least important thing in many weeklies."

You can even lose your story, once you have interviewed its subject.

Judy warns: "Don't think you have a story in the bag until it's been published. Agencies and other freelancers are very ruthless and will ring "your" case study offering to double their money. It's very easy to lose stories this way."

Lastly, once you have filed, never forget that these magazines are no place for writers who are precious about "their" copy. It may come out word for word but with no by-line, or perhaps it'll appear chopped and changed, with your name and that of a staff writer.

The cheque, at least, will have your name on – so keep smiling.

But when will that cheque arrive? Sally says payment can be a major hassle.

"You're not paid most of the time until publication. If your case study decides to back out, there's no kill fee. Ensuring my case studies are happy is by far and away the most important thing to me and that's not just being altruistic. If they drop out, I'd lose a packet."

And what about showing off your fantastic work? Forget it!

"If you're in any way motivated by seeing your name in print in these magazines, don't bother. Your name might run alongside the story, but the copy can be re-hashed beyond recognition by an in-house writer," says Sally.

"Once you accept that the magazine are essentially paying for your 'idea', not your writing style, it's easier to handle."

Louise Bolotin is a freelance journalist, whose first experience of writing for the 'real life' market is not one she would like to repeat. She hopes other writers can learn from what happened to her.

"I was commissioned to write a highly personal piece on my experience of having a cheating husband," says Louise.

"I was offered £400 for 800 words, which I considered to be a reasonable fee, and I was given a by-line.

"I found it quite hard to get the emotions down on paper, but, with some guidance from a journalist colleague who specialises in personal pieces, I did it. I filed and then had some follow-up emails from the subs' desk asking for a bit more detail here and there. So far so good.

"But I was appalled when the piece appeared. They'd sent a photographer round to do shots of me and I hated the one they used. But far worse was the alterations made to my copy. I don't mind being subbed for house style or copy being cut – these are to be expected. But essential facts had been altered.

"I got an apology and an admission that they should have sent the subbed copy back to me for clearance after making such huge changes, but I had to wait a week before the online edition was altered and, of course, I could do nothing about the print version except console myself that it would be fish and chip wrapping fairly quickly.

"My advice to others considering 'real life' work is to be very clear that, once you file your copy, it stops being yours in a way far beyond losing control over any other kind of copy you file."

So that's the downside. Sounds pretty tough doesn't it? If you are determined to forge ahead in the 'real-life' genre, then I hope these down to earth pointers help you steer your course to publication. But there are massive benefits to working on these types of stories, just one of which is that they can help change people's lives.

## WHAT STILL WORKS?

What sorts of subjects are needed for a successful real life pitch? The way I'd put it is, say, anything that has happened in real life, but this begs the question "can it really have done?"

Examples from my real life portfolio include:

I married the best man

My Boxing Day hangover was triplets

Walking tall: I'm so proud of you sister

## WHERE DO YOU FIND SUCH STORIES?

Again, it's a matter of getting out and meeting people, putting the word around that you are looking for stories and what sort of stories you're looking for. Personally, I wouldn't advise taking stories from local papers or small news websites as there might be other freelancers or agencies chasing the same stories. Beat the competition by finding your own.

Get to know the characters in your local hairdresser, laundrette or corner shop. Take time to chat and see what crops up.

## STEP-BY-STEP: A WOMEN'S MAGAZINE FEATURE

Breaking into the highly paid, so-called real life market can seem daunting for a number of reasons. The nature of the stories covered isn't for everyone, and the level of personal details needed can prove off-putting for those who don't fancy asking such potentially difficult questions.

Here's my step-by-step breakdown of what happens next:

1.  There should be no pressure and no offence if the subjects of the story change their mind. These are personal stories and you can't go ahead without their permission.

2.  If they have already been featured in a mass-market publication, then you won't be able to place their story.

3.  Use brief information to put together a pitch to the magazine. Ask them for a picture from a family album, scan it in and send it with your pitch or get a jpeg. Supply the basic details a magazine will want. These are: the ages of everyone in the family, full names, full address and dates of birth (those last two not for publication) and occupations of all members of the family.

4.  Send your pitch and a picture of your case study to the editor to give him/her an idea of the person whose story you are telling. If this is your first foray into this sort of market, then send it to one editor at a time. If you are more confident that it's a great tale, it might be worth your while trying several at once and plumping for the best offer.

5.  The editor would come back saying whether he or she wanted the story and, if so, what fee would be paid to both you and your interviewee – who might be referred to as your "case study".

6. He or she would send you a contract, which the case study signs, promising not to talk to other media until after the publication.

7. Once you have submitted your story, which you should write according to the publication's guidelines, it might also be added to by a staff writer. Do not be disheartened, unless they do a full rewrite and ask a load more questions! You have done your job so long as you have provided compelling, legally sound copy, which answers all the questions the magazine's readers may have.

## TRAVEL WRITING

Would you like to sample a luxurious hotel before bashing out 1,000 words and jetting off to your next destination?

Forget it. The biggest misconception about travel writing is that it's an easy way to make a living, says author, journalist and trainer Dea Birkett. "You have to do other things to pay the mortgage," she says.

"Unlike other jobs, you have to be on duty 24/7. It's exhausting. When you're white-water rafting up a New Zealand river, you're also watching yourself do it. In effect, taking notes about yourself. No-one else on the raft – unless it's jam-packed with travel writers – is doing those two things at once. They're just holding on.

"You might trek around Kenya for a week but then come back to your electricity bill.

"It's a week away. A day or two to organise the trip, then another day to write the feature. That's about 10 days for maybe £500."

"Wannabe travel writers need to be realistic about what lies ahead," adds Dea, who says: "The newspaper and magazine market is shrinking, as more sections rely on 'readers recommendations', for which they pay nothing.

"The trend is away from 1,200-word features towards listings, which are compiled in-house. Most people now go to the web for their travel writing.

"Newspaper websites all pay less than print pages, so again, income is decreasing."

Freelance travel writer and commissioning editor Vicky Baker also urges caution: "You have to remember that the same rules of freelance pitching still apply. It sounds obvious, but, for some reason, people often overlook this in travel.

"Some of the least convincing pitches I've seen come from experienced writers – 'I've written for X, Y and Z, and I'm going away to Barcelona. Would you like a piece?'

"You need to offer an angle – preferably involving something new, topical, little-known or a inside perspective."

It makes sense to keep travel writing as a sideline.

"Perhaps try the odd travel piece for an occasional market – one with long lead times to accommodate inevitable rewrites," advised travel editor and journalist William Ham Bevan.

"Those wanting to get into travel get fixated on the supposed glamour and prestige – one to remember when you're bored rigid in front of BBC World on hotel cable.

"They forget that they're likely to be paid on the same linage rate as any other writer. So you might get the same amount for the same number of words as the bloke doing a feature on, say, wall plugs; but your piece necessitated a five-day trip rather than an afternoon of phone interviews and 30 minutes on the cuts file."

If, after reading this, you are still determined to give it a go, then Will has some valuable advice: "It's the informal relationships among travel journalists that are really worth fostering. The clearer the idea freelancers have of what each editor wants, and the editors have of what each freelancer is capable of delivering, the more likely that a match will come up."

"And remember, you should always pitch a story, not a place."

## TIPS FOR TRAVEL WRITING

Here, journalist and author Catherine Cooper shares her top tips and some guidance with us. Catherine has written about travel for newspapers, magazines and websites.

Catherine also has her own fantastic blog at Travelling with children. (http://catherinecooper.wordpress.com)

- Don't think that you have to go somewhere exotic to write a great travel piece. It's fine to write about a day at your local park or museum or caravanning holiday where it rained all the time. It's what you bring to the piece that is important – not where you go

- Don't feel you have to write about everything that happened on your trip – this is an article for other people to read, not a diary

It can work to pick one element of your trip and focus on that – for example, I recently wrote travel pieces based on a didgeridoo lesson in Utrecht, Holland, a theme park based in a nuclear power station in Germany and a seven seater bike ride – also in Germany. And along those lines…

- If you spot something quirky on your trip, write about it

- Use your own voice. Don't try to emulate someone else, or write how you think a travel writer should write. However, remember you are writing for others to read – not for your own amusement

- Accentuate the positive and don't dwell on the negatives – especially minor gripes. People tend to read travel articles to find inspiration for their own trips. If the hotel was grotty, mention it but don't dwell – perhaps write about the fantastic beach instead. But, alongside this…

- Be honest

- Try to find a different angle – for example, I recently wrote about a trip to Disneyland, Paris, with a guidebook that aimed to cut queuing time. To me (and to most editors) this makes a more interesting article than "My trip to Disneyland"

- If you found a great restaurant/bar/beach, recommend it – but don't write about every single place that you ate

- Include relevant details at the end – how much the accommodation cost, how to get there, websites and phone numbers for booking

# Research and Interview Skills

*" Being an author is like being in charge of your own personal insane asylum. "*

Graycie Harmon

# Chapter 6
# Research and Interview Skills

These are exciting times for writers, as swathes of information become accessible and digital publishing gives many people, who have previously largely remained silent, a chance for their voice to be heard.

The internet is full of amazing opportunities for research, collaboration and news gathering. That doesn't just mean typing something into Google – even though so many of us do. There's a wealth of other ways of searching online, of finding reputable sources, catalogues, archives and more, plus effective tools to help you make sense of what you find. If you don't know what Yahoo Pipes are, for example, now would be a good time to find out.

Check out work from journalism lecturer Paul Bradshaw, on what, to some, will be a mind boggling array of applications designed to boost or support journalists' research capacities. User Generated Content is at the forefront of much of the media we now consume.

But it also presents a lot of problems.

In chapter 4, pages 79–80, I mentioned how important it is to make sure your story is true and recounted how a supposed survivor of 9/11 hoodwinked many journalists and readers. I also listed some of the checks you can carry out to avoid this happening to you.

A more recent example of an internet hoax also illustrates how easily we can be fooled.

When a blogger went missing in the spring of 2011, her disappearance quickly became a cause celebre on the internet and in the media. Amina Arraf was praised for evocative dispatches about the Syrian government's opposition to protesters. When she was reportedly seized by security forces, the US state department launched a probe. A concerned world looked on to see what had become of her.

Trouble was, it was all made up. Lesbian "Amina" was really a 40-year-old academic called Tom, living in Edinburgh.

Media outlets were duped and wrote about the trials and tribulations of the 25-year-old, as she mused about her life and criticised the regime of Syrian President Bashar al-Assad.

This hoax raises awkward issues about how much we rely on online information and social networking for news reporting, how much we trust what's written and take things at face value. As reporters, journalists or writers of non-fiction, we can't afford to fall for such untruths. People behind hoaxes have their own agenda and will welcome the interest of a gullible writer.

It's your job, as a writer commissioned to contribute a news story, feature, opinion piece, book review, or anything else, to make sure it's rooted in fact. Imagine what could happen if someone you included in your copy was found to be non-existent, or events they reported were untrue. How would you feel if you were the one to believe them and tell their story first or to have copied someone else? What do you think your editor would say?

### WHAT CAN YOU DO TO AVOID SUCH A SCENARIO SULLYING YOUR REPUTATION?

My response may be simplistic, but, after 20 years in journalism, it's the only one I can give – don't rely on the internet too much for your information. Back up everything you can with hard facts found in real life. Talk to people as much as possible, meet them face-to-face when you can. If alarm bells ring when you get to know a 'online persona' then follow your instinct.

## NURTURE CONTACTS AND GAIN THEIR TRUST

While the plight of a fake blogger may be a thoroughly modern phenomenon, knowing how to research and interview to get the best results is a long established priority for successful freelance writers.

Elsewhere in this book, you'll see that, to make it in freelance writing, the writing is just one of the things you have to worry about – and there's not much room for shyness. The understanding of these two aspects comes together most closely when you are carrying out an interview.

## THERE'S NO SUCH THING AS A STUPID QUESTION

Ask it, you will look a lot more stupid if you can't explain something because you haven't found out for fear of looking naïve or foolish, especially to your editor.

Think you don't know enough about a given subject to write well about it? Nonsense! Reporting skills mean you can research the subject and ask the questions that matter to a mainstream audience.

For example, if you are writing about technology, the article is likely to focus on what the technology allows you to do, rather than the ins and outs of the technology itself.

On my training course all those years ago, I was told "there's no such thing as a stupid question." I still agree. As the interviewer, I'm not trying to dazzle the interviewee with my knowledge of the subject; I'm representing the readers so I make sure I ask all the stuff they will want to know.

Put yourselves in their place; they might not know what all the jargon used by your interviewee means and they aren't as close to the subject as whoever it is you plan to include in your piece. If you don't understand an answer, nor will the readers, so take great care to make sure what you're writing is clear enough for everyone to understand.

## HOW TO MANAGE AN INTERVIEW?

Telephone, face-to-face or by email?

From my experience, the best interviews are done face-to-face, so that you can observe your subject's body language as they respond to your questions. You can see how they fit in with, and relate to, their surroundings, you can put them at ease more, learn more about their life from what they choose to surround themselves with, and take in the atmosphere! You can also challenge them and react more naturally to their responses, by taking the conversation in any direction that fits, however unexpected, but still make for a better story. This can't be done in a Q&A session over the phone or by email. The more effort you make with your interviews, the more you will get out of them.

Face-to-face interviews can also help you gain confidence and there's no better way to hone your interview skills.

But these aren't always possible and these days, you are just as likely to find yourself chatting, quizzing, or grilling over the phone, as you are knocking on someone's front door.

## TELEPHONE INTERVIEWS

Prepare questions that you must ask, but allow the conversation to develop as if you were face-to-face. There's no point sticking to your keenly crafted questions when your subject reveals a nugget of information that will take your story to a whole new level. Take a deep breath and ask them about what they just said. Go with it and you'll be onto a winner.

## EMAIL INTERVIEWS

I hate these but I still use them, sparingly. Sometimes an interviewee will request an interview by email, or, if you are going to be speaking to them, they'll request the questions in advance. Treat such requests with suspicion. Why would someone want to do that? Put yourself in their shoes: perhaps they are overly nervous and have never met a writer before. Do all you can to put their mind at rest and assure them there is nothing to worry about. I'd politely decline the request to see the questions in advance, unless there were exceptional circumstances – and by that I mean George Michael giving me a private audience! Move over Parky, your time is up.

There is a huge problem with email interviews. Although the interviewee can favour them, all spontaneity can be lost. You can't see their reactions, you can't jump in with another follow up question and you won't have a clue what your subject makes of your interview. It's also incredibly frustrating when a carefully thought out question comes back with a simple 'yes' or 'no' – so my advice is to avoid email interviews unless you really, really can't. At the very least, ring up your subject and talk their answers through.

If you need to interview someone in a different timezone, then you may want to consider an email interview more carefully. But, for me, I would still see what I could do to talk on the phone, just for my own peace of mind that I was getting all that I could from the conversation. If I interview someone in America, for example, it may be nighttime at home, so I will take time off in days to come for staying up. Why shouldn't you? Or, of course, I may just lump it!

## RECORD YOUR INTERVIEWS

In 20 years of journalism, I have twice been asked to produce a shorthand note of a conversation I've had. Both times, despite complaints about being "misquoted" by the interviewee, the editor has been happy with the accuracy of my notes.

I'm an old fashioned sort and I would very much like to recommend that anyone considering being serious about a freelance writing career learn shorthand. But I know that's not going to happen.

But you still need to record your interview and there are a host of funky (and not so funky) devices on the market to help you do this.

Do take notes too. My memory of a health conference in Birmingham circa 1999, isn't great and nor was it by the time I came around to writing about it as the deadline approached a couple of weeks later (not an approach I'd recommend!).

Thank goodness for my pages and pages of notes, when my first and only attempt at using a Dictaphone failed spectacularly. The Dictaphone worked all right – there was just far too much background noise for me to make head or tail of what the speakers were saying.

There are also devices to record telephone conversations that I have seen heartily recommended by fellow freelancers.

If you are going to use any of this technology, don't make the same mistake I did in not checking out how best to operate the equipment. Don't leave this to the last minute, and always make sure you have enough charge left to avoid an embarrassing power failure as your subject looks on or chats away.

## HOW DO YOU START?

Take time to make your interviewee feel comfortable. I do this by explaining, once again, who the piece is for, when it's likely to be published, how many words I'm writing, and what angle I'm hoping to take. You can, of course, choose to chat about the weather instead. It really doesn't matter, in my opinion, so long as you put them at their ease, instead of launching in sounding like a grand inquisitor as opposed to someone wanting to help tell their story.

## PREPARE YOURSELF

But putting them at ease means more than smiling and being polite. Also take time to find out as much as you can about them before you meet them. When they see the care you have taken to do this, and how this informs your questions, they are bound to feel more open to those questions than those of someone who just turns up and hopes for the best. Similarly, thinking about and planning what you are going to ask will always be in your favour. You may want to ask what you consider your most important questions first, if time is tight or, you may feel you want to build up with simpler lines of inquiry.

## BACK TO BASICS

I remember being interviewed on the phone as a mum who was willing to speak about healthy eating for children. Glossing over the fact we were in Kentucky Fried Chicken at time, the journalist (Lucy Jolin) said to me first off, confidently but gently, "Let's get the basics out of the way first," before proceeding to ask me if she could check the spelling of my name, where I lived, how old I was, what I did for a living, what my partner does and how old the kids are. Phew! I was really impressed – up until then I'd always left this 'belt and braces' information until the end of an interview but these days would heartily recommend Lucy's approach.

## GO ON – TALK!

Ask open questions – not ones that can be batted off with a simple 'yes' or 'no'. Don't make your questions over-complicated; help the conversation flow. If you get an inkling that your subject isn't comfortable, take a moment to find out why this is. Then you can decide whether to make them feel more at ease or plough on regardless (Sometimes it'll be your job to nudge them into telling you things they might not want to give away!).

Again, if you really don't feel right about asking awkward questions, please consider whether this is the right path for you. You are far more likely to have your copy thrown back at you because it's full of holes where you should have asked more questions, than being told the writing isn't right. Sub-editors can tinker with copy to make it fit better or tidy it up – they might view that as their job; but they won't be best pleased if you have missed out basic or key information.

## IT'S NOT ABOUT YOU

Listen to what your interviewee says. You may be bursting to tell them the most amusing anecdote in the world as they are talking to you (or perhaps that's just me) but this really isn't the time or the place. For some, there's a fine line between putting someone at their ease and making them feel uncomfortable with irrelevant chit chat or interrupting when they are speaking. You are aiming to be professional, listen to what they say and be prepared to follow up with relevant questions that present themselves on the spot.

## WHAT DO YOU NEED TO KNOW?

Follow your editor's brief, if you have already placed your feature, and base your interview around making sure you find out what's needed. If you are interviewing someone in the hope of finding an interesting story to sell, make sure your questions are open-ended but targeted enough to make that happen.

## INTERVIEWING CHILDREN

While I was researching a piece on bullying for a magazine, a seven-year-old interviewee burst out crying and gave the phone back to his mum. Hardly an auspicious start.

Interviewing children can be a daunting task, not least because of all the ethical and legal considerations. And that's before you have attempted to coax a nugget of a quote out of them.

In the latest version of McNae's Essential Law for Journalists, there's a swathe of information relating to under 16s – from juvenile court cases to a "right and respect for" family life under the European Convention. Journalists at every level should keep up-to-date with shifts within these fast-changing parameters.

The Press Complaints Commission's editorial code of practice also offers clear guidance on what is and isn't acceptable in pursuit of an interview with a child.

Included in the points are:

- Young people should be free to complete their time at school without unnecessary intrusion;

- A child under 16 must not be interviewed or photographed on issues involving their own or another child's welfare unless a custodial parent or similarly responsible adult consents.

In reality, the most pressing issue can be how to get your interviewee to actually say something and – even better than that – something that adds to your piece.

## UNDERSTANDING

A journalist and editor, who was also a school counsellor, told me you have to make sure young people fully understand what you are doing and be prepared for them to possibly change their mind.

She says: "Open-ended questions can work well in these circumstances – it may take longer to get what you want, but they are far less threatening and you're not putting words into their mouth.

"Children tend to want to please and are used to doing and saying what adults want, so they can feel pressured and you can end up supplying them with the answer, if you're not careful.

"Under the United Nations Convention on the Rights of the Child, you should also be mindful of protecting the child's best interests.

"This means that you should bear in mind the consequences for them of printing anything they may have unwisely said.

"It's also a good idea to explain to them that their view is crucial to the article – that you value their views and you aren't just 'using' them. It is somewhat unethical to include their view merely as 'decoration'."

My colleague at Passionate Media, Helen Moffat, is a former chief reporter at the Wolverhampton Express & Star and has also written for education titles.

"Where it becomes difficult is when the story is about a tragedy they have been involved in, and you are asking them to relive something painful," she says.

"Children can also often include lots of irrelevant details in stories, too, and need a bit of steering back onto the subject."

Helen agrees about putting the child at ease.

She says: "Ensure they are somewhere comfortable and accompanied by an adult they trust. It is often more difficult getting them to speak in front of their parents, but you have to find ways of breaking the tension, talking about things away from the subject and lightening the mood."

## LOOK AFTER YOUR CONTACTS: IT'S NICE TO BE NICE!

Journalism is one of the most cut-throat and cynical professions you're ever likely to encounter. To listen to some reporters speak, you'd think they've hated every minute. The miserable old so-and-sos do nothing but moan about declining standards and how it was all so much better in some mythical golden age.

You may feel the same or you may disagree. However you feel, remember that, when dealing with contacts and interviewees, it pays to be professional and approachable.

When I worked in my first reporting job, my colleagues used to rib me about how sympathetic I was to people who rang in with a possible story. Sometimes the caller wanted to moan about the damp in a council flat, sometimes they wanted to tell us about their parents' Golden Wedding, or even about a lost dog.

Some were lonely and appreciated a chat with a daft young woman on their local paper, even if it was to advise that we were banned from writing about missing pets.

As soon as I put the phone down, the laughing would start. "You're not a social worker," my colleagues would chip in.

But it's funny, those same people would ring back, again and again. Sometimes it would be to say they had some interesting background information about a current court case, or that they knew someone who'd just had their 13th child, or was at the centre of an important investigation.

So it was the young "social worker" who found her name more frequently on the front page or her stories in the nationals the next day. I remained in touch with some of these people for years and they became the sources of some more cracking stories or ideas.

So what's the point of sharing this here? Well, I think it's good to remember that you never really know who you might be talking to when you first hear from them. Treat your contacts well and they will help your writing career flourish. Poor 'people skills' can mean professional and financial suicide. Not only do you need to build relationships with people and organisations in your areas of interest (often from scratch), you need to cherish those contacts. And why not cherish the editors too? Now there's a thought. More on this in 'Doing Your Own PR.'

## QUICK T!P

**PUT YOUR HANDS UP**
And when your editor asks you a question about your subject that you haven't sought to answer, don't reply "She didn't say." I hate that with a passion. Far better to admit "I didn't ask, sorry." Yes, you might consider it a little embarrassing but you can be sure to remember it next time.

## THE ANSWER'S "NO", NOW WHAT'S THE QUESTION?

Can interviewees see your copy before you forward it to your editor? "No" is the usual answer, as it's just not accepted practice and you have an accurate note of what they said, and when. You should remain fair and impartial at all times, and that includes not being swayed by interviewees into letting them influence how you are going to report their story or quotes.

## AN EXCEPTION TO EVERY RULE

The most obvious time you can show your interviewee what you have written is when? Well, when they are paying you to write about them, whether it's for a press release, brochure, advertorials or other marketing material. They are the client after all, so it's no good getting on your high horse!

The other time that I might check parts of my copy with its subject is when the story is a very sensitive one. I want the interviewee to feel comfortable and confident at all times that I can be trusted, and may need to check the facts through again if it involves serious illness or bereavement, for example.

## WHERE TO FIND YOUR INTERVIEWEES

Clue : it's not always online.

Click onto any forum for writers and you might find an abundance of "case study requests."

This is a contentious issue.

In my days on a news desk, I know I wouldn't have been impressed with such blatant attempts to crib off other people, expecting to be handed information on a plate.

Now, it seems for many of us, me included, pressures on our time, through home, work, and family, can mean we reach out for the quickest solution.

But there's still a danger, isn't there? How exactly do you know that the contacts you make through the internet are any good? Who are all the other members on a forum and how useful is their advice?

People can mean well but do they really know what they are talking about? And what if they are like the audience on the Russian version of Who Wants to be a Millionaire? They deliberately misled some poor soul when he chose to ask them for their help, didn't they? You do find some mischievous blighters on any forum.

There are even websites dedicated to helping people star in the media, putting them in touch with journalists keen to tell their stories.

## PROCEED WITH CAUTION

You'll also find an abundance of websites set up to bring PR people and writers together. Response Source (**www.responsesource.co.uk**) is the best known. As a writer, you can register and let people know who or what you are looking for to include in your story. Used well, this can be an effective means of communication, so long as the PRs abide by guidance given. Unfortunately, you can also become the target of some seriously misguided approaches once you have aired your request, as PRs bombard you with irrelevant information. Measures are taken to stop this happening so please don't think it will be a regular problem. Used sparingly, Response Source and other websites of a similar ilk may prove efficient for your research, but they are no substitute for doing your own digging and cultivating your own contacts.

## IS YOUR "CASE STUDY" RIGHT FOR YOUR TARGET PUBLICATION?

This is what's technically known as a right can of worms. Increasingly, it seems that people you interview won't make the magazine you are pitching, because they don't look right, whatever their story.

But if you are going to pitch a feature that concerns one or more interviewees, do take the time to find out whether they are of the right age group, social standing or any other criteria to be considered for inclusion in a particular magazine.

Ask many a staff or freelance writer and they can quote you chapter and verse on women's glossies rejecting case studies or even whole features because of what the subjects look like.

In general, for example, certain magazines will say they want 'smart, modern thinking women'. Sadly, that means your interviewee might not be quite right but she could be for someone else. If she's over 40, she may not be suitable, even in the eyes of your commissioning editor.

Writers have learned how to play the game, although it doesn't always feel right. It's up to you if you want to. There is plenty of money to be made from the magazines who don't insist their featured women should be "photogenic", and, to be fair, they often have the best stories.

## DATA JOURNALISM

Sounds complicated doesn't it?

Put simply, it means investigating data.

Using complex, modern data, statistics, forecasts, reports and more, can bring you a wealth of leads for news stories and features about important subjects.

These may go to the heart of government and democracy.

Or it may be that the complicated numbers published by local councils or other organisations aren't really that complicated.

Instead, they boil down to simple, important human stories that need to be told.

Important data can offer lots of clues about how we live our lives and what's happening in the world. It can act as a foil for false claims made by big business or politicians.

Data is regularly published by statutory bodies, businesses, charities and more. Just think of the huge potential for stories, then plan your time wisely to find out more.

The Online Journalism blog, Journalism.co.uk and The Guardian are among media outlets that have pioneered reporting on how you can make the most of new research tools and methods to get to the heart of the matter in data journalism. Using up to the minute applications available through new software or internet search engines may allow you to discover truths, which can make compelling stories for a wide range of possible markets – even more so when applied to facts and figures obtained through a Freedom of Information request.

This is another string to your bow, which boosts your earning power, not to mention making a genuine difference to people's lives. There's an open data movement in the UK that has been at the heart of many of our most important headlines in recent years. Across the world, data also holds the key to some amazing news stories.

Find out about training courses and workshops to help you understand it if this is an area that you can progress in. You'll need to learn where and how to find the data, how to analyse it and how to turn it into an accessible, digestible feature or story an editor will find compelling enough to commission.

This is a growing area and, as we move further away from a traditional media landscape, one that could prove crucial to your freelance writing success.

# Writing for
# the Internet

*"* When something can be read without effort, great effort has gone into its writing. *"*

Enrique Jardiel Poncela

# Chapter 7
# Writing for the Internet

The biggest growth area in writing in recent times, online publications are now rivalling 'dead wood' media as sources of news, information, and entertainment. If you are serious about earning money from freelance writing, then the internet brings plenty of opportunities but also some pitfalls.

Rates may be lower than print publications, even when the website you are writing for is an extension of a newspaper. I've even known the editors themselves to apologise for this. Don't forget that the NUJ has its excellent Rates for the Job resource and that amounts listed can be treated as a minimum.

Some canny writers will weigh up the rate against how long it takes to produce the copy and see that they are satisfied with the deal. If you can write several articles in a day, then this can work out at a decent daily rate.

That means there are plenty of opportunities for new, media-savvy writers, with plenty more to come.

But beware – plenty will want you to write for exposure (nothing!) or for a pittance.

## KEEP UP WITH THE TIMES

Websites, and in particular those from news organisations, are likely to include not only text and pictures, but also possibly video, audio, graphics and animation.

Also, don't forget that an increasing number of people are no longer relying on a static page on their computer screens to bring them their news and features. They might be accessing it via a mobile phone, a personal organiser, an RSS feed, a tablet or a digital TV screen.

And when they do access that information, don't sit back and expect them to have nothing to say about it. You are likely to be writing something for a truly interactive site, so brace yourself for some lively feedback and think about how you are going to respond.

Be willing to evolve as time goes on, but don't ever think you can afford to ignore the basic principles of providing sound, engaging copy on time.

## K.I.S.S – KEEP IT SIMPLE, STUPID!

Why use 50 words when you can use 10? Why use five syllables when you can use two? Keep it simple! Don't make the mistake that, just because your writing is on the internet, you need to get down with 'da yoof'. Clear, concise copy is what counts, not how much irreverence per line.

You should be concise, direct and relevant, hitting your reader with the most important points at the top of the page.

But, as with newspapers and magazines, what you should know is what's relevant to your target audience and what the house style is.

Hook your readers – and don't let them go.

Internet readers are more likely to scan or skim articles, so ensure your copy is going to keep their attention as well as can be expected.

Expect to use sub-headings, bullet points, 'pull out' quotes, 'boxouts' or 'fact boxes' as per the editor's direction. And if you don't understand any of the terms used – then ask (A boxout is a section carried next to the usual text, with some extra information included in it).

## DON'T ASSUME YOUR READERS ARE EXPERTS

Help them understand: explain any specialist terms, don't use big words to show off your knowledge, and don't make the mistake of trying to cram in too much jargon. Make your writing as accessible as possible – that's a good way of writing whatever your medium, but especially so on the Internet.

### QUICK T!P

**KNOW YOUR AUDIENCE**
Who is the site for? How many people read it, of the 500+ million people with access to the internet? What do they need to know and why is what you are writing important to them? Don't assume anything, find out.

## STICK TO THE STYLE GUIDE

You may write "per cent" in other articles, or form the date in a certain way. It'll be different and more concise online.

Most websites have a style guide. Treat it with the respect it deserves. Stick to the font and the way of presenting copy that's spelled out. If there isn't one, then do ask the editor for pointers. They might surprise you with a contributors' guide.

Just like any other reputable freelance market, successful websites will have their own style and approach. Make sure you are familiar with them before you pitch, and follow the right track when you submit your copy.

In addition, there are a number of considerations for writing for the web that need to be borne in mind. They are connected with people's concentration levels and an assumption that they want to access clear information quickly.

Author and mentor Nick Daws offers the following pointers:
Writing for the internet is different from writing from print. There are two main reasons for this. One is that text is harder to read onscreen than in a

book or magazine. And the other is that internet users are typically looking for specific information, which they want as fast as possible – they are considered less likely to be reading for pleasure or relaxation.

For both these reasons, text written for web pages, emails, and so on, should be as quick and easy to read as possible. Here are five tips to help you achieve this:

Break text up into short sentences and paragraphs. On a web page, or in an email, five lines is about as deep as you should go.

Make each paragraph a self-contained statement, and ensure that the statement is worth reading. Remember that bored readers will be on another page with a click of their mouse.

Use plenty of headings and sub-headings. These help break up the text, and show readers the structure of the document they are reading.

They also provide handy reference points for navigating the document and reminding readers where they are in it.

Use bulleted lists wherever possible. Bullets are easy to read online and, in well-written copy, each one provides a concise morsel of information.

Allow plenty of white space. Even in printed copy, long, slab-like paragraphs of densely written text are off-putting, and that applies doubly (at least) online. Using short sentences and paragraphs, headings and bullet points will all help create more white space, of course.

Nick has produced a downloadable course called The Wealthy Writer, which is co-written by Ruth Barringham. It's all about making money writing for the internet.

Find out more at www.nickdaws.co.uk/wwriter.htm.

## ONLINE RESEARCH – BE CAREFUL

People can hide behind a computer keyboard to make up all sorts of stuff, as some pretty nasty court cases have shown up in recent years. Check the details and then check again. If you find a possible interviewee via the internet, do all you can to make sure they are who they say they are. And if you read something that could be worth a mention in a piece you are working on, then make sure you can 'stand it up' by more traditional means, say, by digging out the details of anyone concerned and checking directly with them.

## FEEDBACK AND BACKCHAT

I'm an ignorant Socialist whose brood is robbing taxpayers of their hard-earned cash. And I write lazy, boring, pointless rubbish. I'm sexually confused and an "aspirational chav".

These are just a few of the choice comments writing online has brought me, in comments on my articles. What fun.

When this happens, I laugh. It doesn't bother me – better to be talked about than ignored, as many people would say.

But sometimes the comments can turn even more personal. These should be removed by moderators.

Author, journalist and tutor Ellie Levenson told me such barbs are an expected, and partly accepted, irritation.

She says: "If writers worried about this kind of feedback, we'd never write. We should be more worried when there is no response at all.

"The internet allows people to give instant and often ill-considered responses, which can be aggressive and offensive. I operate a 'don't engage' policy, though I'm always interested in considered comments – whether they agree with me or not."

Ellie says commenters may not realize how they come across.

"Tone is notoriously difficult to get on an email and I think it's the same for online comments," she says.

But whatever you do, don't write for a site where you can see how harsh the comments can be, if you're in no doubt you'll be upset. If you do, choose whether you are going to engage in debate about your article or not. I would love to, but often the comments are so vicious or the commenters so entrenched in their prejudices, I think better of it. It may be that you are expected to comment, your editor should advise on this.

## MASTER YOUR OWN DESTINY WITH A BLOG

You can use a blog to reach out for new stories, help with your research and build trust with readers. A blog can also showcase your writing and earn you money independently of other freelance work.

No blog is an island. If you're covering a particular field in your blog, then you can be at the forefront of that specialism. That means you can keep up with current research, stories from around the world and other developments. This gives you the opportunity to also pitch ideas to editors. Of course, they may say "no" – they frequently will – but you are at least upping your chances. Not only can your site highlight your knowledge, it can also reach out for new stories and help with your research.

A blog I used to run about twins and more (www.gotyourhandsfull.com) helped me build trust with readers – mostly parents of multiple-birth children. They contacted me with stories that not only made their way onto the blog, but also into the pages of newspapers and magazines. I included my email address, and an appeal for people to get in touch with their stories, on the front page of my blog, and now and again reminded them in a new post.

How you request information or stories can require a lot of thought – make sure those who answer understand what will happen at every turn. It's no good getting a bite from an editor, only for your interviewee to then cry off with the excuse "I didn't know I'd have to be named". As with the wider world, not everyone who reads a blog knows or cares how newspapers and magazines work.

Another important element to bear in mind, if you ask for stories through your blog, is making sure that the people who get in touch are who they say they are – ensuring the story's "copper bottomed" as a few of my ex-bosses would say. With the sort of human interest stories I was working with, I may fix up to go and see the person who got in touch, I may already know them or I'd carry out all the usual checks needed to stand up such a story – talking to any third parties and authorities involved.

Journalist and blogger Craig McGinty warned against straying into unfamiliar territory – onto other people's blogs, for example, especially when they are already at the centre of media focus. He says: "Some people still don't realize that, unless they make their blog a private space, then it is open to search engine spiders and can be found. After the Virginia Tech shootings, journalists flocked around one or two posts trying to get comments. It looked ugly and despite seeing many requests from reporters – and the backlash – more requests were left, including some from journalists based thousands of miles away."

Craig adds: "The principles you'd use when interviewing someone, regardless of how you are doing it, should be followed. Be courteous, understanding and get the facts right."

You can also point editors to your blog when you pitch. Journalist and blogger Diane Shipley says: "Blogging has been very good for my writing career. Co-editing Trashionista (www.trashionista.com) gave me the clout to write about chick lit for The Guardian's books blog. Writing for my blog, as well as professional blogs, meant I was offered commissions out of the blue – one for Mslexia and one for The Telegraph.

"I'd pitched both editors before but it was my blogging experience that interested them, and led to other work. I recently had a piece published in Company. As I'd moved house and changed phone number and email, the editor had no way to contact me – I'd sent the piece in on spec, six months earlier, and forgotten about it. So she looked me up online, and left a comment on my blog saying they'd like my permission to publish it. I'm glad she did!"

## EMBRACE THE BLOGOSPHERE

Understand what a blog is – that's an easy-to-update website. Although the 'easy' bit is important, the key element is 'update'.

Get one for yourself. They are free through **www.blogger.com** or **www. wordpress.com** and cost a few pounds a month through **www.typepad. com**.

Not only can a blog showcase your writing, it can also help you develop your style of writing for more online markets.

In the past, people found it difficult to update their website as it usually involved asking another company to place the new text on the site and often a fee was charged.

Not surprisingly, websites quickly become static entities with very little information beyond contact details, an overview of the business, and a list of services.

But the internet never stands still, and although this type of site might have been suitable in the past, search engines now look to highlight websites that offer fresh articles and are talked about on other sites.

The old five or six page static websites are sadly lacking these key elements.

However, blogging software allows you to easily update your site, automatically sets up links to new articles on your site, enables readers to ask questions and tells both search engines and followers of your writing that you have written something new.

## BANISH YOUR PRECONCEPTIONS ABOUT BLOGS

No, they really aren't just online diaries.

Well, sometimes they are of course. But you will find some beautifully executed blogs. They can be much, much more than a collection of random thoughts or pictures.

## UNDERSTAND HOW YOU CAN BENEFIT FROM A BLOG

It's important to stress that you'll only enjoy success with a blog if you are willing to give time to writing articles.

If you think you can build a meaningful presence with an entry once or twice a month, then you need to see if you can expand on that. It is possible but you would be making things a lot harder for yourself.

Some of the benefits include:

Your website will establish you amongst your peers as a person who follows your subject, provides an online resource where both your own experience and that of others can be found, and allows interested readers to follow your writing. This establishes you as a commentator in your sector and so you gain strong benefits and presence elsewhere.

Another key benefit is that you are pre-qualifying visitors to your site, as many will arrive at your website via a search engine. People often turn to search engines with a question in their minds and it is the job of the likes of Google, Yahoo! and MSN to find an answer.

Because your site is often updated, has clean and simple links to your articles and is easy for search engines to find, then, if your site provides an answer, you will feature on the results page.

So already, that person has seen something that might well answer their questions. When they read an article, or find other pieces that highlight something that they had not thought of, and your blog gives them the option to post a question there and then, there is a good chance you will have developed a quick link with this person.

The comments being left by people are also a benefit because they will point to problems and questions that visitors have, and so provide you with an insight into a need. Consider it free market research for article ideas.

## CLINCH THAT BOOK DEAL OR TV GIG!

Yes, really. A blog can unlock a great deal of potential. Publishers and agents have been known to scour the internet for unsigned writers with an original voice, people who can entertain and inform, provoke debate and build a loyal following. There are several bloggers who have hit the literary heights. Remember though, these people are the exception rather than the rule.

Or promote your blog's niche interest by establishing yourself as an authority on your chosen subject. I've been contacted many times by editors and researchers wanting to chat on air about a specialist subject, thanks to a relevant blog I've launched.

## IF SOMEONE COMMENTS – COMMENT BACK

When readers find your site, you want to ensure that they feel part of it and let them interact with it in some way. The ability to leave comments on a blog site is another feature that makes them stand out from regular websites, but it is the feature that most worries people.

Thanks to your blogging software, each article can have a comments feature so people can add their own thoughts, leave useful advice for other readers or ask you to clarify something.

Comments on your site show that it is an ever evolving spot on the internet and it can soon build up to provide tightly focused information on individual articles. They are also very helpful for search engines.

Some of the most popular blogs are those with busy comments sections, continually generating snippets of text on a particular subject.

As a small aside, some of the biggest websites on the internet are those that allow users to create the pages for them. If you think about eBay, people actually pay to update the site! Similarly, if you let people leave comments, your site is receiving new text without you actually writing anything.

## DON'T WORRY ABOUT NEGATIVE COMMENTS

Your blogging software will allow you to moderate any comments being left by people so that you can cast an eye over them to see what they say before allowing them through onto your site.

But a word of caution – don't use this moderation facility to ignore questions posted by disgruntled readers.

Consider allowing a debate to unfold in your comments, this can add a great deal in terms of interest.

If it turns nasty, though – take action and consider removing incendiary comments from troublemakers, known as trolls.

Remember, search engines register as many websites as they can and look for useful articles to help answer questions.

So if someone posts a complaint through the comment facility and you fail to act on it, they could easily write about their problems with you on their own website, going so far as to detail all the steps they took to try to sort them out.

Their moan would no doubt feature your name, allowing search engines to pick up on this. This is a poor reflection on you, and all because you failed to act upon one comment.

You can turn negative comments around to ensure any damage is kept to a minimum and even show you acted swiftly to ease your reader's worries. One way would be to publish their comment and then, directly beneath, write a reply saying what you will do.

Another course of action could be to write a new article (blog post) about the person's complaint, indicating what you did to help them out, and how you have changed things within your business to try to make sure something similar doesn't occur. After all, we are all human and make occasional mistakes. Showing people how you have dealt with a situation is a great reflection on you.

Finally, with all these new articles going on your blog, you want to be able to tell readers when there is something for them to read, without relying upon them to remember to visit or pop your site in their 'favourites' folder.

Blogging software will have the facility to publish something called an RSS feed, which is a way for your website to tell people you have something new for them to check.

If a reader of your site is interested in following what you write, they can ask their feed-reader to check your site's RSS feed and tell them when a new article is published. So when you next post a piece, your new site visitor will get a message in their reader, and, with one click, they can be reading your latest article.

## SEARCH ENGINE OPTIMISATION

Regularly updating your blog, and gaining new links from other sites discussing or sharing your content, will help search engines find you. You can monitor where your readers come from with the use of free systems such as Site Meter or Google Analytics. Which of your posts are most popular, what search terms are leading people to your blog? This is all precious information to help you make the most of your blog but also provides wider insights that can help you shape future feature ideas and commissions for paying markets.

## THE STYLE GUIDE BEGINS AT HOME

If you are looking to make your blog work hard for you and boost your business, then it needs to look professional.

Not only should you study paying publishers' style guides carefully, you should also adhere to one on any website or blog to showcase your writing.

The design and style is something that you most probably take a lot of time over, but what about the words themselves? It is important that your articles look as one, that readers are not confused by the appearance of the words on the screen and that your audience is comfortable reading what you write.

## HOW TO BLOG: CONTENT IS KING

Ex-Midlands features editor Tara Cain has around 40,000 readers a month on her blog, Stickyfingers (**http://stickyfingers1.blogpost.com**)

She says:

### Write what you would like to read

I like there to be a reason for a post, a story – I suppose I like it to have a start, a middle and an end. I hate 'today I was doing this' sort of posts, or long rambling ones with nowhere to go, because I find them boring. I suppose that's the editor in me, but I like the post to have purpose.

### Good headlines are important

The journalist in me says, if something doesn't have a magnetic headline, I'm unlikely to read it unless I love the blogger and then I'll give them the benefit of the doubt!

### Include a mix of posts

Some could be long and introspective, others short and sweet, some may be made up of photos, while others could be funny and some sad.

- Don't talk about yourself ALL the time

- Don't ramble

Eva at Nixdminx: **www.nixdminx.com**

## Throw out the rule book!

I've been writing professionally, either as a PR, journalist or blogger, for 20 years. Frankly, I just can't help myself and I've always kept journals.

When it comes to blogging, for me there are two camps; journalists who write on specific areas and journals from consumers who write for the love of it. My personal blog is very much a journal style and writing it over the last year has been a complete education in itself. So what I've learned is that, for blogging, you write your own rules. It is your personal space and place to do with what you want and how you want to do it.

*If you're starting out and are keen to find a voice, there are some tricks which may help;*

**Do you have a digital camera?** Take snaps of something that catches your eye and write a story about it.

**Has something made you howl with laughter?** Capture that story, add conversation, build up the suspense by setting the scene; what day was it, where were you, why were you in that situation, how did it flip into something funny?

Perhaps there is something happening in your world that has been written about in the media – do you have an opinion on that? Do you agree or disagree or sit on the fence? How about you get your point across and write about it on your blog – you owe it to yourself, and other people may want to get involved in the conversation with you.

Finally, I think it really does work to get involved in blogging carnivals, many of which are themed and help lend a starting point to the topic you will be writing on.

Blog editor Camilla Chafer (**www.camillachafer.co.uk**)

## What's in a name?

A name is one of the first things that is going to grab attention for your blog and if you want to register it as a domain name, you're probably going to have to be quite inventive, as most easily thought of names with popular domain suffixes (.com, etc) will have already gone. Think about what the keywords would be to describe your blog and play about with them until you've coined something that sounds right, feels right and is available for registration.

## Finding a niche and are there any niches left?

Yes, most topics have been covered but there's always a new angle to look at. Even if there is competition within a niche, if you can do it better, it's worth a shot.

## The design

When you launch your blog, it should look as professional as possible. It is your shop front, the thing people first register before they even start reading your sparkling content. Fortunately, many blog platforms have templates that can be used and can be played about with to gain the colours, format and fonts you prefer, all with minimal design know-how. Try and have the design exactly as you want it to be from the launch so that readers aren't confused by sidebar features that appear one day and disappear the next or ever changing templates.

## The right tools

Equally important, if you're blogging for an audience or for profit, is to have your analytical tools in place from the beginning. You should register with sites like comprehensive blog directory Technorati, sign up to Google Analytics to understand your traffic, where it comes from and what it does when it reaches your site. Register the site with search engines.

## When should I launch my blog?

When it looks good, when it has a name, when it has some content and when you feel ready to share it with the world. Also take into account any industry events that might be going on that will help you gain your blog readers from the get go.

## Be prepared to wear many hats

If you're lucky enough to work for a paying blog publisher, they'll cover design, marketing, promotion, advertising and more.

If it's just you, you'll have to learn how to do it all, from creating the site and registering a name to finding advertisers, spreading the word and creating all the content. Don't be daunted, learn these valuable new skills and enjoy seeing the fruit of your labour as your blog becomes successful.

Tips from Erica Douglas, from the free Ace Inspire Business Blogging e-course **http://www.aceinspire.com/aceblogger-ecourse/**

## Pick a niche

Choose a well targeted niche that is wide enough to give you a sensible customer base but narrow enough that you can make your voice heard.

## Become an expert

Build your credibility by blogging, writing for journals and websites, speaking at conferences, and so on. Use social media to raise your profile and become the 'go to' person in your chosen niche. Create a press page where you can share your coverage. Consider writing a short eBook on your chosen expertise – anything to demonstrate your pre-eminence in the niche.

## Build your audience

Drive people to your blog from other social media platforms. Attract traffic from search engines by creating regular high quality content that will help you rank well. Encourage reader engagement by asking questions, having an option for commenting and engaging in discussion.

## Choose your monetisation strategy carefully

Different monetisation strategies will work for different audiences or niches. If you have a lot of traffic, sell banner advertising. If you have an audience that likes to buy then consider affiliate marketing. If you have an audience that has a thirst for education in your topic, then create eBooks and eCourses to satisfy this. Of course, your niche may suit a blend of these.

## Paid advertising on your blog?

Camilla says:

Pro-blogging can pay. Not always, but certainly sometimes. If you have a blog that produces excellent content on a regular basis and is attracting readers, you might be able to earn some money.

Revenue is gained through advertising and there are plenty of advertisers that will place ads on your blog once the blog has been approved as worthy and it's actually quite easy to do.

Some rely on page impressions, some on click-throughs and some on a sale only basis. It all depends on the advertiser and your blog's popularity as to how much, if any, money you'll make.

Here are some popular advertisers to get you started:

Google AdSense – These ads can be embedded on your blog in a variety of formats.

Tradedoubler – Small image and advert texts from a variety of household names.

Widgetbucks – Adverts for leading names.

**Affiliate links** – check your favourite stores to see if they have an affiliate setup. For example, Amazon's affiliate advert can be placed on your blog and if it is used to perform a search and subsequent sale, you'll receive a percentage.

Check your favourite blogs to see who their advertising is provided by and do some research. Try out different advertisers and find out which ones are profitable for you.

Bear in mind that many blogs don't earn anything and others make enough to enable the bloggers to concentrate solely on their blogs. For the first few months, you may earn nothing at all and that's when many give in.

Don't expect the earth in terms of income from your own blog. Use it as a platform for pitches, speaking engagements and more. You are in control, work hard enough at it and your own blog can bring massive opportunity.

### CHECKLIST: BLOG POST

Tick off all of the following to make sure your blog post is as attractive as it can be:

The heading: Make sure it is easy to find on the major search engines.

Link, then link some more: Link to outside sites that interest you and are mentioned in your piece, but also link to previous posts on your own blog – they're a long time in your archive and it will increase time spent on your site if your readers have more of a mooch around. Include related post links with your latest piece.

But don't make links that pro-blogger Craig McGinty calls "speed bumps" – so many links they just get in your way.

Be topical: Write about that burning issue, today, not next week! The conversation will have moved on.

Keep it short, simple and, if at all possible… entertaining: Who's going to come back to a blog that is as dull as ditchwater?

Use multiple categories: Increase the chances of your reader finding your post in the future by including it in your blog's different categories.

Use Technorati tags: These will show you who else is discussing the same stuff.

Keep up with the conversation. Drop by their blogs too and leave a comment, who knows, they might come and check you out, too.

Enable comments and trackbacks: It's good manners to listen to your readers – and to respond to them, too. It might be time-consuming, but you want to interact, don't you? Else what's the point?

Include an excerpt: For anyone keeping up with your blog through a feed as opposed to clicking onto the home page.

Stick to the same style: Be consistent. Find your style for names, dates, etc. and stick to it. Anything else looks sloppy.

Don't overlook images – but be aware of copyright: Use your own pictures, request publicity shots or ask permission. You wouldn't want someone to rip off your words, so don't rip off other people's images.

Break up longer articles into shorter posts: Extend your post to get more page impressions.

Also: Read through all the pointers in the newspaper article checklist and make sure you get to grips with most of that, too – especially understanding libel.

background
MULTIMEDIA
websites
microblogging
DIGITAL
WWW
email
CLOUDS
info
NETWORKING
BLOGGING
illustration
advertising
WORD
telecommunications
HUMAN
information
connection
global
WIDE
typographic
WEB
SOCIAL
INFOTEXT
world
blue
relations
MEDIA
CONCEPT
internet
GLOBE
black
touch
interaction
ADVERT
RELATIONSHIPS
BUSINESS
text
COMMUNICATE
podcasts

# Social Media
# for Writers

*" I love writing. I love the swirl and swing of words as they tangle with human emotions. "*

James Michener

# Chapter 8
# Social Media for Writers

There is massive potential to forward your freelance writing career with savvy use of social media platforms.

You can still write features aimed at print publications, and, with a bit of adapting, you can be podcasting and blogging, too.

You can get some training or learn as you go along while working for established blogging companies. Then you'll be in a position to set up your own blog on niche subjects.

This will help you build up a specialism, and it's a double whammy. You can make money off your own blog and also build a name for yourself as an expert in a specialist subject, and this can broaden your publishing output.

How social media has helped me diversify and survive.

Overall, I'd say that a growing knowledge of social media has allowed me to:

- Survive and diversify in my chosen career

- Make new contacts I never would have met previously

- Improve ways of finding, researching and completing existing work

- Find new income streams – both directly and indirectly through blogging but also in offering my services to help others get to grips with the concept of social media and understand that it's not about technology for the sake of it

- Better promote my work across various disciplines

As an 'old school' journalist, it has been very interesting for me to see how that career path has changed and how social media is further shaping the new media landscape.

These days, as a director of an agency, I've had to diversify to survive and social media has been at the very heart of that survival. I have sought out ways to add to my skills, forge new contacts and relationships and make money using a variety of social media means.

## FIVE TIPS FOR UNDERSTANDING SOCIAL MEDIA

I've encountered many writers who are suspicious or scared of getting involved in social media. In part, this can be down to their level of knowledge or understanding of what it's all about, or they may worry about any negative connotations.

They want to know how much time it needs and what their return on investment will be.

Here are five tips I reckon are small steps to help demystify social media and make it work for you.

Anyone calling themselves an expert or guru, probably isn't. This is such a fast-moving, emerging phenomenon that there's already lots of noise made by people trying to make a quick profit by persuading others that there are rigid rules governing the use of social media, and their way is the best or only way. But, as I hope the following points help show, that isn't really the case, save using a bit of common sense.

Don't be blinded by the technology, remember that this is quite simply a way of communicating. Yes, really, it's as simple as that. I am quite possibly the least technically proficient person you could meet, but even I can find my way around Twitter and the blogging platform Typepad. I'm currently learning Wordpress, which I'm assured is even easier.

Quit concentrating on how long you are worrying it takes and think about the benefits. Of course, it is going to take time to build up a meaningful presence on social media. But the benefits are huge. Sounds obvious doesn't it? And well, I would say that. But again, think of it as a means of communication. If you are passionate about your message, isn't it important to get it out there?

People buy off people, even online. How many times have you heard business people utter a version of this somewhat immortal cliche? Quite a few, I'd be willing to bet. So, when you venture into social media, remember that just as you wouldn't steam on in in real life, to scare people witless with an aggressive sales pitch, nor would you do this in a social media environment. Relax, be yourself and be interesting. Give people a reason to follow or engage with you – that's what counts.

It's all about community in real life, how do you interact with contacts? If you attempt to pummel others into submission with your amazing sales pitch every minute, nobody will want to talk or listen to you. But you can also find contacts, learn interesting stuff and share news of what you're up to when you meet real life contacts. Crucially, you also listen to others and may even do them the odd favour! The end result? People know you and your services, you build a community around them. It's exactly the same with social media. Sounds easy, doesn't it? Why not give it a go? You may just find it is…

## TWITTER

Twittering or "tweeting" used to mean telling everyone who's interested your answer to the question 'What's happening?' The 'What's happening?' question has since been dropped. You can also send messages direct via Twitter – but they have to be 140 characters or less. Log on at twitter.com to get started. An array of journalists are already having their say in a public timeline.

You can update your feed and read other people's tweets and messages, either online or via your mobile phone. What you say, and how often, is entirely up to you.

Inevitably, opinion is divided on whether this "micro-blogging" service is useful. Fans maintain Twitter is a great way of keeping on top of important developments, while detractors insist it's all a waste of time. Do we really need to know what someone had for dinner, again?

But Twitter can be about much more than that. Major news organisations, including the BBC, Al-Jazeera and The New York Times, keep followers up to date with headlines.

When I wrote about Twitter, as it was getting off the ground for the journalists' magazine, Press Gazette, I interviewed senior tech journalist Chris Green.

He told me then: "It's an effective news distribution and promotion mechanism, and I'm using it to point people towards interesting content online and offline, as well as flagging up issues and concerns for discussion.

"It's a great ice-breaker. New contacts will say they've seen my Twitter feed. Larger news organisations using Twitter provide a cheap, near real-time and multidevice way of being kept in touch with important and breaking news."

Chris said those slating Twitter for some of its more inane messages are missing the point:

"There is a lot of more sensible use – and some very worthwhile and interesting conversations going on. Anyone who reckons it's a waste of time should at least give it a go to see the bigger picture."

As a freelance writer, I have gained ideas and leads for pitches from stuff I've read on Twitter and, as a news junkie, I know my next fix won't be long in coming.

Another way that you can shape Twitter to your best advantage as a writer is in promoting your work. But beware, too much self-promotion and people will switch off and stop following you. Share your links sparingly – not 20 times a day.

A popular use is to add a link to your latest article, which can help underline your specialism or find new readers.

Whether Twitter has any bearing whatsoever on developing writing skills is, of course, debatable. Can you edit your thoughts into 140 characters or less?

## HOW TO TWEET

In your profile, make sure you have:

- A photo

- Your web address

## WHEN YOU TWEET

- Be concise

- Be accurate

- Be compelling

## WHAT TO TWEET

Twitter says: "Compose new Tweet…"

Your tweets can be on anything.

You don't have to talk about what you had for breakfast, though some people do.

## DO:

- Link to interesting content – from you and other people

- Mention what's happening now

- Offer advice

- Pass on opportunities

## DON'T

- Repeatedly share the same content

- Ignore people

## FOLLOWING AND UNFOLLOWING

Following does not mean stalking

- Build up slowly

- Find people you want to follow

- Follow them

- Follow their followers

- Engage

- Look out for Follow Friday – people recommend others to follow and should say why

- Don't be scared to unfollow someone

- Don't obsess over someone unfollowing you

- Be mindful of spam

- Be mindful of 'bots' – weird sites set up to automatically retweet certain words: Thank you, sssh, etc.

- You can block people

- You can report abuses to Twitter

## REPLYING:

Reply as you would in real life:

Say thank you

But don't obsess over not replying if you don't have time.

How to see your replies:

Go to your Twitter homepage

On the left hand side, click on @

## DIRECT MESSAGES

You can send and receive them, so long as both parties are following each other.

Don't be tempted to automatically DM someone with a marketing message when they follow you. This is frowned upon because authenticity is key.

## HASHTAGS

You may want to use a hashtag for research purposes or to take part in a conversation on a given topic. A hashtag is the following symbol: #

Their official description is "a community-driven convention for adding additional context" to tweets.

But the best and simplest way of understanding them that I have seen is likening them to Post-It notes.

## FACEBOOK

Some people find it highly amusing that freelance writers have their own pages on facebook, where others can click to like them or become fans. Others find it depressing when journalists market themselves in this way. I consider it a fact of life and get on with it as one more way of raising a profile with the aim of forging professional relationships and finding work.

This is easier for me to say as I do this under a company name. I'm not sure a "Linda Jones" fan page on facebook would be something I'd like to see.

But that brings me on to a relevant point. These pages are separate from your personal profile. Find your own way on facebook – many writers make facebook friends with colleagues, customers and contacts, others consider it more of a personal space. Which do you prefer? I left facebook after amassing more than 500 'friends' as (I'm sorry) some of them weirded me out a bit – they called themselves freelance writers and sent me requests to meet up in London and chat, they wouldn't take no for an answer. I came back and am now mainly 'friends' with people I know in real life.

But a group I set up for my blog at **www.freelancewritingtips.com** worked well – allowing me to publicise workshops and alert members of freelance opportunities. Groups are now pretty much outdated in a lot of people's eyes and pages for communities or businesses have taken over.

Facebook is continually changing. Find out how it can work for you and make your own way. Perhaps you want to link to published articles or use it for research.

You can maintain both a personal and business presence on facebook by making sure your personal privacy settings are as strict as possible. This means people who decided to like you on your business page can't see anything you post to your personal profile. And if they send you a friend request, you can decide whether to accept or ignore. Or you can send a message thanking them and politely and tactfully letting them know that your personal profile is the sole preserve of closest family and friends. In this case, you can suggest they follow your business page to keep up with your work that may be relevant to them.

Facebook provides clear instructions on how to set up pages. Check out what other writers are doing and see if you could benefit, too. If it's not something you want to bother with, then many would say that's perfectly understandable.

### HOW TO UPDATE YOUR WRITING BUSINESS' FACEBOOK PAGE

- Invite people to join but don't spam

- Find your own way

- Be concise

- Be professional

- Be realistic – don't get addicted and update too often – you want people to see you do actually have some work

- Don't rely on communication through Facebook, make sure you follow up through other means, to check details or credentials of people who get in touch, where needed

## LINKEDIN

Unlike Twitter and facebook, LinkedIn is powered specifically for business, so it doesn't have the potential of blurring boundaries between your professional and family or private life. With millions of users, it serves most industries and professions.

You can join groups on LinkedIn to help in your career, ask and answer questions and build a network. You can pay to sign up for a more advanced version. If this appeals to you, ask around to see what benefits people have found after doing this and if you remain unconvinced, don't part with your money.

The best aspects of LinkedIn for me has been former colleagues getting back in touch and the capacity for customers to provide recommendations, known as testimonials, which are visible to anyone who may check you out on LinkedIn.

## MY EXPERIENCE OF SOCIAL MEDIA

### Blogs

You've got your hands full

I blogged about twins, triplets and more here. I started this blog to help parents find more information to help them, as I felt there wasn't enough awareness about the unique challenges they face. Three years on, I was proud to say that I had a US editor for the site and reached 11,000 returning visitors at one point. But the individual messages of thanks and support I get from readers mean a great deal more than the stats about readers, which can fluctuate a lot.

The blog enhanced my career as the trust built up with readers has meant they have come to me with stories I have been able to sell to high-paying UK publications, as well as helping with research for commissioned features.

## Freelancewritingtips.com

This site is regularly updated with hints and tips about freelance writing, it includes interviews with freelance journalists and copywriters and relevant features from printed publications I've written for.

## Havealovelytime.com

I'm very excited about this new blog. This is a collection of travel reports by parents for parents. Interest in advertising to support the site has been encouraging.

## Passionatemedia.co.uk/speakingup

As part of a role as a media adviser with the mental health charity Mind, I set up this site to help people tell their stories. This led to writing for One in Four magazine, as well as being featured in various national publications.

## TWITTER

I'm @LindaAitchison on Twitter and have around 3,500 followers. Just as I have been delighted at the opportunities blogging has brought me, I've been chuffed at the way I have been able to forge and build relationships online through Twitter.

Most importantly, I was made aware of a specific regular part-time editor's role, which was highlighted solely through Twitter.

My interest in Twitter began as I wrote for a now defunct Shiny Media blog called Twitterati. Like other social media platforms, it also provided food for thought when it came to pitching newspapers and magazines. I subsequently wrote pieces for The Guardian, Telegraph and Press Gazette about Twitter.

## PODCASTS

My partner is a former BBC journalist, most recently working at BBC Birmingham online and Midlands Today. We are now working with a number of commercial and not for profit clients on podcasts to help them spread the message about their products and services.

## FACEBOOK

We have facebook pages for our company and some of our blogs. We use these to send out messages to people who have shown an interest in what we are doing and to alert them of upcoming events and opportunities. It has been heartening to hear that some writers have gained freelance work through updates sent via this means.

## WHAT HAVE I LEARNED?

I've always tried to see the 'bigger picture' and think long term when presented with opportunities in my career, so have enjoyed embracing social media and what this has brought me. I've particularly appreciated the 'social' aspect as I have built not only professional alliances but friendships, too.

## MY ADVICE

I often read tips about using social media from 'experts', 'gurus' and consultants.

I couldn't claim to be a guru by any stretch of the imagination but, as someone who has experimented for themselves, learning as I go, as well as advising others, here are my top five tips:

## BE YOURSELF ONLINE

Don't try and be someone you're not. Be open and honest. Above all, be sociable. Networking online is the same as networking face-to-face in many ways. You'll meet people you adore, people who make you want to bang your head on your desk and many inbetween. Relax, be yourself and engage. Help people out. They may do the same for you one day.

## BE CONSIDERATE OF OTHERS

I know it sounds obvious, but it never ceases to amaze me how inward looking (okay, self-centred) some people can be. If someone goes to the trouble of commenting on your blog, sending you a message on Facebook or tweeting you in response to something you have said on Twitter, why not reply? I know people are busy or that now and again they just can't be bothered. But to be constantly broadcasting and not listening or engaging, is a pretty poor show in my opinion.

## RELAX AND DON'T TAKE IT TOO SERIOUSLY

Don't get caught up in spats online that you would walk away from in real life. Do you really need to go back and respond to that carping tweet or blog comment again? The answer's probably no, move on!

Be open to new opportunities, but don't turn off your inbuilt bullshit detector.

Check out anyone you want to do business with in the same way you would offline. Don't get your fingers burned.

## GET A LIFE

If you blog about a passion, don't let blogging about it get in the way. Erm, that's it.

## SOCIAL MEDIA AS A RESEARCH TOOL FOR WRITERS

On Twitter, you can use the hashtag #journorequest to appeal for information that could help you with a latest piece of work. This can be very effective as others re-tweet your request. Or you can contact specific people to ask them. You have to weigh up what you want to say publicly and if Twitter is an appropriate platform to ask such questions. Some will be opposed to this. Just as they wouldn't take a call from you, they often aren't likely to respond to a tweet.

You can also use hashtags to search for latest tweets on a given subject, for example, #mentalhealth and locate Twitter lists that bring together people and organisations with a common interest, to keep up with new developments in that field by following its members.

Journalists now often quote tweets from public figures in their articles. It seems some UK celebrities only have to pop on to Twitter and the innermost thoughts they express there are splashed across bestselling media. So it would seem that pronouncements made on Twitter are fair game – even if they are later deleted. But still do your utmost to research diligently and not quote people out of context.

Keep up with latest guidance and thoughts on online research through Journalism.co.uk and the Online Journalism Blog. Again consider contempt and libel laws where necessary.

Similarly, you can broadcast who you need to speak to for a feature via facebook or find special interest groups who may be able to help you.

These are just some quick examples of how you can use social media for research, there are lots more and it's a fast moving world. Do yourself a favour and attempt to keep up with it.

## JARGON BUSTER

Blog: short for web log. Some may say an online diary. But a blog can be any website published through blogging software

Feed: same as RSS (see below)

Feedburner: site/service allowing you to add a feed to your blog to deliver your content to readers without them having to log on to read it

Follow Friday: Twitter initiative where tweeters recommend others to follow – and should explain why – some calls for it to be done away with…

Google reader: service to bring feeds from your favourite blogs together to help you read them in one place

Hashtags: created by adding # on Twitter – terms invented to add to tweets on a given subject and build a community of tweets towards a 'trending topic'

Meme: seen by some as similar in nature to a 'chain letter' circulated online. Bloggers invent them and ask others to take part – then tag others to do the same, creating links to their blogs in the process

Ping: short for packet internet gopher. It lets content aggregators, such as Technorati, know when a blog has been updated

Permalink: link to a blog post, link to this to enable your blog readers to track the influence for what you have written/relevant information

Podcast: audio file made available online

RSS: Really Simple Syndication. Delivers internet content to subscribers

Social bookmarking: tagging, storing and sharing internet content

Tag: a descriptive label used to index content

Technorati: blog search engine, currently undergoing major changes

TinyURL: website/service providing less cumbersome links

Trending topics: most popular subjects on twitter in a given period of time

Tweet: to publish something on Twitter or a noun describing a message published on Twitter

Vlog: a blog where the content is provided in the form of video Web

Wiki: website allowing users to edit and control content

2.0: The second generation of web where online content is created, collaborated on and shared by the community

# Other Types
of Writing

*" You write to communicate to the hearts and minds of others what's burning inside you. And we edit to let the fire show through the smoke. "*

Arthur Polotnik

# Chapter 9
# Other Types of Writing

If you're someone who feels they simply have to write, then chances are you may also want to spend time on more creative endeavours than writing for newspapers, magazines, websites or commercial clients.

If you feel you have a chance of being the next Maeve Binchy or Ian McEwan, then seek out other aspiring writers in a similar genre, allow yourself time to write and finely hone your craft.

You may want to start with short stories and exercises. Get to know your strengths and weaknesses, gain constructive feedback from colleagues at real life writing circles or online sites.

## FICTION

### Find your own voice

Be original, write from the heart and edit with your head.

Advice from Keris Stainton, author of Della, says OMG and Jessie (hearts) NYC

Here are some questions and answers from Keris, with her opinion of what it takes.

### WHAT CHARACTERISTICS DO YOU FEEL A WRITER NEEDS TO 'MAKE IT'?

Determination would be the big one. It's taken me a long time to get to this point, but I never thought about giving up because I have to write. I don't feel like myself if I'm not writing.

## WHAT ADVICE DO YOU HAVE FOR ASPIRING WRITERS WHO WOULD ONE DAY LOVE TO BE WHERE YOU ARE NOW?

Join a writing group. I hated the idea of a 'real world' writing group where I might have to read my writing out to other people, so I founded an online group and it was one of the best things I ever did. In fact, after hiring Suzy Greaves, it was the best thing. Not just for feedback on your writing, which is, of course, incredibly useful, but also just for chatting and encouraging and sympathising and asking stupid questions.

## HOW HAVE YOU MANAGED TO FIT YOUR WRITING IN WITH YOUR USUAL WORK AND FAMILY LIFE?

I'm incredibly lucky in that I have the easiest kids in the world. Joe sleeps for three to four hours every morning and Harry did the same (he's now at school). I also have a very hands-on husband, who is not only happy for me to disappear to the computer when he gets home from work, but who also cooks. Work-life was a bit harder because, for a while, it was the journalism that was paying while the fiction was just a dream. But now I tend to focus on the fiction in the hope that the harder I work at it, the sooner the rewards will come.

## WRITERS' BLOCK – REAL-LIFE PROBLEM OR IMAGINED HURDLE?

Well, I'm a strong believer in the power of the imagination, so I'd say it's an imagined hurdle that becomes a real-life problem when you focus on it.

## WHERE DOES YOUR SKILL IN WRITING COME FROM AND WHAT HAS HELPED NURTURE IT? HAVE YOU EVER BEEN ON A CREATIVE WRITING COURSE, FOR EXAMPLE?

I don't know how to answer that question because I don't believe I have a skill in writing. I'm not trying to be modest, I'm genuinely shocked when people say that kind of thing. All I try to do is write as naturally as I can. But, no, I've never been on a creative writing course; I would be far too self-conscious. I did do an online writing for teenagers course a few years ago (run by YA author Lauren Barnholdt) and that was brilliant for my confidence and for finding two fabulous crit partners (Sara Bennett Wealer and Darcy Vance), both of whom have since got book deals, too.

## FIND SOME FRIENDS

Visit your local reference library or ask around to find out when and where a local writers' group meets. Read Writers News, Writing Magazine and Writers' Forum to keep up with latest opportunities and advice, as well as regular competitions to test your skill.

Also, check out the vast range of online resources for wannabe novelists and story tellers. There are regular weekly opportunities for flash fiction online and flourishing networks of forum members who will read and comment constructively on your work. I've relished advice given on My Writers Circle. There are lots more, have a look around and see which you could feel at home in.

I've had great encouragement, have been published, and am now working with a published author of women's fiction as a mentor thanks to contacts made in these supportive online environments. My work has also been met with encouraging noises from agents, thanks to my presence on writers' forums, which is a great confidence booster.

But the advice that keeps coming back to me, time and time again when I fantasize about completing a novel: Just write the thing.

## SHORT STORIES FOR WEEKLY MAGAZINES

Unfortunately, this, too, is a shrinking market but opportunities still exist. One of the best resources I have found for keeping up with chances of publication is the popular Womag Writer blog **http://womagwriter. blogspot.com/**

## GET THE STYLE RIGHT

Your story needs to have pace, it needs to flow well and having a sting in the tail may be the best approach. Buy the magazine you are aiming for and see what stories they are carrying, could yours be as good? Request writers' guidelines to help you head in the right direction.

## PLOT MATTERS: KNOW YOUR AUDIENCE

Create contemporary characters with whom readers can relate and empathise. Help readers laugh with your heroine or feel for her.

## AVOID THE FOLLOWING HACKNEYED PLOTS:

Animals telling the story

Twins playing tricks

Existing partners brought together by a matchmaking service or website

Kelly Rose Bradford, who featured in chapter two, lists the following as favoured scenarios. But remember, of course, they all need a fresh take:

- Marital disputes

- Challenges of bringing up teenagers

- Spouses taking each other for granted

- A new arrival

- Battles of the sexes

- Sibling rivalry

- Holidays from hell

- Families at war

- Betrayal

- Current markets

At the time of going to press, a campaign was under way to save Coffee Break fiction in Take a Break. Check out the Womag Writer blog for up-to-date guidelines for other markets.

## THE DEVIL'S IN THE DETAIL

Adhere to guidance from the magazine on how to submit your work. If they ask for a certain font, stick with it and double spacing is likely to be required.

## NON-FICTION BOOKS

There's a huge market for non-fiction books and if you have developed a successful specialism, producing a book to underline your expertise and advance your career can be an excellent idea.

But earnings from such works can be very low. Agents will not be interested in representing you if the advance is likely to be low, as it is in most cases.

Fancy trying your hand at a spot of non-fiction book writing? You have a corker of a subject in mind and can bash out a knockout synopsis. So what's stopping you?

The trouble is, for every Jon Snow or Andrew Marr, there's twice as many writers turning out works for small presses whose sales, to put it politely, aren't going to set the world alight.

These aren't the esteemed writers whose works excite the chattering classes, but jobbing freelancers whose aim is to help their career and hopefully earn a few quid along the way.

If you are considering writing a non-fiction book because you would like to make a fortune, then you need to reconsider.

Think what else having a book published can bring you. If you are building a specialism, then having a book or two under your belt is a real boost. Then there's the relative longevity of such a title – books may be cherished by readers far longer than a piece in a magazine, newspaper or website. So where to start?

Ghostwriter and author Andrew Crofts advised me that it's better to have an agent.

"Agents help you shape the sales pitch, know which publishers are in the market for what, and can nearly always get the price up higher," he says.

Yet, in an increasingly competitive market, persuading an agent to take you on is easier said than done and you may be better off approaching publishers directly.

Former Rough Guide editor, Fran Sandham, clinched a deal for his travelogue Traversa by the tried-and-tested method of writing to publishers listed in the Writer's Handbook.

## MONEY MATTERS

When it comes to money, you may have heard that you can get an advance, royalties or both. What are the sums involved? Don't book that cruise just yet. An advance may not even be offered, or may be the equivalent of one 500-word piece in a national magazine.

Seek advice. Talk to the Society of Authors.

You should also take into account the difference in "culture" between the industries of journalism and publishing. Freelance journalist and author of The Girls' Guide to Losing Your L Plates, Maria McCarthy, says that writing a book is a "much bigger deal."

"Don't think it's going to be a breeze. Writing a book is a much bigger job than writing a series of articles," she says. "You can get bogged down in research, underestimating the time to actually write it up, thinking that the writing will just happen one day."

You also need to be prepared to work hard to push your book.

Yours is one product among many, and unless your book takes off quickly, they may soon forget about it. Have your own marketing plan.

These days, that includes blogging, Facebook and Twitter. In the absence of a massive PR machine, word of mouth can be key. Even established author Crofts turned to YouTube, uploading a trailer for his book, the Overnight Fame of Steffi McBride.

## GHOST WRITING

Other people's stories can be a good source of income, especially if you are already well versed in spinning a good yarn as part of a magazine short story or feature. You may not be able to get past a celebrity's 'people' to negotiate a deal with them as a newbie writer but look out for local people who have been caught up in an extraordinary chain of events. They may have had their name cleared after a miscarriage of justice or been the investigating officer in some high profile crimes. If they have overcome a great deal of adversity or featured in national or international news stories, then there may be a market for a book about them and you could be the one to clinch the deal, thanks to the right combination of news sense, grabbing the opportunity and pitching an agent or publisher.

## HOW TO PRESENT A SYNOPSIS

Make it as compelling as possible, just like a pitch. Research and follow specific guidelines from publishers. Be prepared to set out, if requested:

- Title

- Concept

- Proposed content

- Chapter breakdown

- Sample chapters

Author credentials: Include relevant experience of published writing and full details of any previous books (title, publisher, date, sample reviews perhaps).

Competing books: Who will you be up against and how will your book differ?

Market for the book: Who will read it and why?

Promotional possibilities: Include anything you can do and contacts you may have to help promote the book (Often, with small publishers, the more you can do the better).

Delivery: How much have you already written and when will you have a completed manuscript?

## WRITING FOR THE STAGE AND SCREEN

Check out specialist resources and training to turn this dream into a reality. The best thing you may be able to bring to a proposed project is insight gained through already reporting on a hard-hitting or many-faceted story for a media outlet. Perhaps you could pitch a TV production company or help with further research. It's a crowded field but, as with any other part of writing, you only need one yes to get you started.

## FINDING AN AGENT

I know writers who have been approached by agents out of the blue, following radio interviews they've given or blog posts they have written. This is just yet another sign of what can happen when you market yourself effectively but it's by no means the norm.

The Authonomy website from Harper Collins, where fellow users appraise your story, has also been lauded as a site giving power to readers as opposed to agents, with author Miranda Dickinson famously being snapped up. Again, caution is needed.

If you network effectively with other writers, you should be able to ask for recommendations about agents. Attend writing events and conferences where you will be inspired and attain professional feedback and criticism on your work in progress, as well as more of an idea about which agents may be right for you.

Study agents' websites and blogs where they publish news and views about what they are looking for. Research well-thought of books in this area, subscribe to the Bookseller for insider information, as well as Writers News for announcements of agents striking out on their own and explaining what they're looking for.

So you have the Writers' and Artists' Year Book, you have the internet and you are stocked up with back copies of your favourite writing magazines. So how are you going to find an agent? It still comes back to networking – ask other people who you trust. Find the right forums, blogs or groups online and you may even find published authors who are willing to advise you. Many writers are now also on Twitter – if you can build up a rapport with them via social media, at some stage you may be able to seek advice, so long as you aren't too pushy, choose your time wisely and think carefully about what you ask. Don't expect too much, these are busy people.

## PUBLIC LENDING RIGHTS

The UK PLR Office distributes money to UK authors based on how many times their books are borrowed from public libraries.

All UK authors are eligible for PLR so long as you have registered with the PLR Office at www.plr.uk.com.

Nick Daws says: "I've made literally thousands of pounds from PLR payments. Some books have earned me more money this way than in publisher fees or royalties."

It's also imperative that you find out about the Author's Licensing and Collecting Society (ALCS) and how this body can help you earn more money from your published books.

## SELF-PUBLISHING AND E-BOOKS

Self-published authors say the days when 'vanity publishing' was the norm are long gone. They argue that battling against the frustrations of working with commercial publishers needn't be the only route to success as an author. They suggest that, contrary to popular belief, because print on demand providers assess work purely in terms of literary quality rather than commercial viability, the standard of such books is, if anything, slightly higher.

Bloggers and social media aficionados also laud self-publishing for the opportunities it brings. Selling books off the back of your blog can put you firmly in control.

## QUICK T!P

### BEWARE OF SCAMS
Small scale magazines about writing and websites for the aspiring author may include ads for self-publishers, correspondence courses and get rich quick schemes that seem too good to be true, promising all manner of riches. When something seems too good to be true, it invariably is. Do your research, find out about credentials and never part with money up front, however small the amount.

## A BEGINNER'S GUIDE TO E-BOOKS

Joanne Mallon says:

'E-book' is a slightly strange word, which stands for electronic book. Rather than a traditional hard copy of a book, the reader receives a file that they can either print out or read on a computer screen or via a specialist e-book reader.

These days, e-books are usually read on an e-reader as opposed to a computer screen. E-books can benefit from all kinds of multimedia gubbins – hyperlinks in the text to relevant websites, video clips, etc.

Authors are using e-books in an increasing number of ways to directly sell or promote their work, sometimes cutting out the need for a more traditional publisher altogether. Amazon Kindle versions of e-books are selling like hot cakes.

So why did I decide to write an e-book?

Well, basically, because I could.

The process went like this:
First I wrote the words in Microsoft Word.
Then my technical department (AKA partner John) packaged it up into e-book format.

I promote it through my professional networks, website and blog. PayPal takes care of the payment processing. When someone buys the book, they get directed to a secret squirrel corner of the internet where they can download it straight away. I wake up in the morning, an email tells me that somebody's bought my book, I take the money and spend it on chocolate. Easy, anybody could do it.

Before writing my e-book, I had already spent a lot of time on a book proposal for a book about getting a job in media. I wrote about 10,000 words, bunged in all my best Richard & Judy stories, and genuinely thought that no publisher would be able to resist its charm.

Well, whilst the proposal did attract some interest from publishers and agents, it never actually secured a publishing deal. As a busy, working mother, I live by multi-tasking. I simply don't want to waste that kind of time again, writing something that might never see the light of day. I'm not somebody who just writes for the love of writing – I write for the love of people. I hope that people will read my book and find it useful and entertaining. I hope they can learn from my experience. I hope it makes them smile. But none of this will happen if the dang thing never gets published.

At least with e-books, like other forms of self-publishing, whether or not it's going to be published isn't in question. The author has control over the whole process from start to finish. And you keep 100% of the royalties, as opposed to around 10% as is the standard publishing deal.

From a business point of view, it also made sense for me to have a lower priced product. I'm a professional life and career coach, specialising in working with people in the media. Not everybody wants to, or is able to, spend £200 on coaching, but they might spend £20 on an e-book.

Also, I am quite selective about the limited number of one to one clients I'll take on to coach. But there are no limits to the number of people who can buy my e-book, so it spreads the reach of my work much further than I could do as an individual. It provides a taster of what I have to offer as a coach, and some of the people who buy it do later go on to become coaching clients. So it's a marketing device as well as a useful book (hello multi-tasking, my old friend).

And there are other advantages that are peculiar to electronic books:

- With an e-book, delivery is instant and automated. No more trudging down to the post office because the postie couldn't fit your Amazon parcel through the letterbox.

- The publishing process is speeded up immensely – you could write an e-book one week and be selling it the next. And there's no hanging around for royalties either.

- You can set your own cover price – many e-books are given away for free, but I have seen them priced at up to £100 for specialist texts. As yet, there's no established norm.

- E-books can be updated easily and at any time – no need to sell a load of old stock before you can issue a new edition. In fact, there is no physical stock.

- As a 'virtual' product, there's no issue with storage space and the supply is unlimited.

- No trees will have to be sacrificed to print your book.

- The e-book format means that the number of pages are necessarily shorter (how many pages do you want to read onscreen?), so it's a good format if you want to focus on one particular topic, which would not be suited to a longer length book.

- It's a useful promotional device, so you can easily include a copy when you sell other services.

- It doesn't preclude you publishing a hard copy format – in fact, it can promote it as people who buy the e-book may also buy a hard copy.

- If you're thinking of writing an e-book:
  Do enlist the help of others. Whilst there's an attraction in being able to do it all yourself, every book benefits from several pairs of eyes who'll spot things you missed.

- Think about how you will promote and sell your book. Many e-books are sold using text-heavy, sales-letter type, one page websites. This seems to work well for the US market, but may not if your book is aimed at the UK.

- Research your audience – are they already buying e-books? My book sells mainly to coaches and personal development professionals, a sector familiar with the e-book format. If your potential audience finds the idea of a book you can't hold in your hands too weirdy, you'll have a hard job convincing them to buy yours.

Ultimately, the plan with my e-book was to sell plenty, then approach a traditional publisher with evidence of an established market. I haven't quite reached optimum level yet, but it keeps ticking over. I'm currently experimenting with publishing selected extracts on my blog, whilst still keeping the full e-book available to buy.

# Commercial Writing Work

*" If I'm trying to sleep, the ideas won't stop. If I'm trying to write, there appears a barren nothingness. "*

Carrie Latet

# Chapter 10
# Commercial Writing Work

As a skilled writer who wants to earn money, you can be flexible and assign yourself a wide variety of paid tasks. The rate for so-called commercial writing work can be much higher than 'bread and butter' journalism in some cases and massively more than traditional rates paid for new fiction.

Of course, no amount of money is worth it if it doesn't sit right with your soul, but my view is that there is work out there to be had and it can greatly ease the feast and famine of freelance life.

## TASKS COULD INCLUDE:

- Copywriting for website, brochures and other marketing material

- Compiling and editing printed or email newsletters on behalf of paying clients

- Providing copy for media relations campaigns

- Possibly implementing those campaigns, calling on your skills as a writer or journalist to do so

- Writing speeches, quizzes or awards submissions

- Compiling case studies and testimonials for use in marketing material

- Preparing advertorial

- Helping with sales letters

- Writing material to be used across social media platforms

- Possibly implementing social media campaigns

- Preparing and editing scripts for podcasts and videos

- Maybe providing consultancy services in social media

And, for any of the above:

- Proof reading

- Subbing

- Editing

If a potential client hasn't got the budget to pay for any of the above, then another option would be to provide training in writing skills, however formally or informally, you felt would genuinely fit your experience and their requirements.

You could also contribute media training sessions, if this is where your expertise lies.

### WRITING STYLE:

Are you ready to be subjective?

Can you bring the excitement the client wants about their product or service to your writing? They want you to help sell their products or services and may feel a piece akin to a news story may fall a little flat. Either invest in training in how to do this properly, find a client who loves your writing style or step away.

### A QUESTION OF ETHICS

Some writers will argue that continuing to work as a writer for media outlets alongside commercial clients automatically compromises your status. Or they just won't fancy it.

I can see where they are coming from but I don't agree. I have worked on all the tasks listed above and I cling to a belief that my work elsewhere, as an editor or feature writer, hasn't been adversely affected. The two don't necessarily clash, and, when they do, I take steps to ensure I remain as objective as possible or remove myself from the equation.

But you may prefer to decide which parts of commercial writing are for you and stick with them. Perhaps you could work on website and brochure copy but feel media relations or tweeting would be a step too far.

Be clear on the differences between what is journalism and what is PR at all times and be as transparent as you can in dealings with all clients – commercial or editors.

## IN AND OUT OF THE DARK SIDE

I was asked to do some work at a PR company after having my children. I was totally against it. But the flexible hours, better pay and fun and non-controversial clients I would be working with tempted me away from the subs' desk of a regional newspaper.

At that time, I made lots of mistakes. One of the biggest was treating clients like I was a journalist. While this undoubtedly helps in media relations work, you also have to take on board that elements of PR work, like behind the scenes organisation, project management and, most of all, customer care, are a totally different ball game.

## IS IT POSSIBLE TO DO BOTH SIMULTANEOUSLY SUCCESSFULLY?

Yes – so long as you act with integrity and don't allow the two to clash. So, for example, in my case, if I am responsible for media relations for a local hospice, beauty therapist or manufacturing business (as I am), as far as I am concerned this has no bearing whatsoever on my ability to pitch an editor with a totally unrelated story – say a real life piece for a women's magazine or a piece about social media or mental health – these are diverse subjects and, for me, lines between PR and journalism aren't crossed.

I think there's more of a difficulty when you specialise in copywriting or media relations in a certain sector – it must be hard, for example, to do PR for a car company and be a motoring journalist. Many would consider that a clear conflict. There are times when you can clearly see there's a possibility for the lines to be blurred so you have to act accordingly and maintain your independence as a PR or journalist.

So, for example, if you are working with a charity on PR and they have a campaign highlighting certain case studies – you are not in a position to pitch an editor about those case studies.

You are not objective and this is unethical. In these circumstances, do your PR job properly and step back, get a staff journalist or fellow freelancer interested.

Don't attempt to work anywhere near PR if you know it's going to make you miserable.

Don't assume that, for a journalist working in PR, you have to constantly weigh up these ethical questions – you don't – it depends who you work for, when and how much, both as a PR and a journalist and what your involvement is. There is plenty of editorial work that may come under a PR support or media relations umbrella that you could do brilliantly, without having to write a single press release. And your role can be pretty anonymous if you want it that way – not to hide anything but because it's no big deal in the scheme of things.

As the media landscape shifts, many writers are grappling with similar issues.

Recognise that your skills as a journalist bring lots of what your commercial clients will call 'added value' to your services. If you are worried that you won't cut it, cast your mind back to any of the instances where you have seen poor media relations in action and take heart from knowing you can do so much better.

You must be clear on the difference between PR and journalism and where the potential conflicts of interest are.

## BE TRANSPARENT AT ALL TIMES

Don't pitch an editor about a commercial client as if you are an objective journalist.

Either tell them straight that this is a story you hope they may be interested in on behalf of a commercial client, or don't pitch it at all.

Instead, find a fellow freelancer you trust and see if they can take it on.

You won't be paid by your target publication, but you are being paid by your commercial writing client.

The lines can become blurred when you unearth an idea for a story that isn't directly connected to your current commercial writing job, but still concerns your client, or perhaps someone you have worked for in the past.

If in doubt, flag up any connection to your editor – they can decide if your past or present commercial connections bar you from writing something that may touch on someone you have worked with. Papers such as The Guardian have clear rules on this.

## PRECONCEPTIONS ABOUT COMMERCIAL WORK, INCLUDING PR

Don't assume because you sometimes work in PR that your esteemed editor will think that means you are a prat (I did once and they didn't). There is a growing recognition that, for many freelance journalists, working in media relations/commercial copywriting is an increasingly attractive or unavoidable option.

Be clear on the differences of working for an editor and working for a commercial organisation as their PR person or copywriter – there are working practises, systems and procedures outside of the media that mean you have to shift your mindset, adapt and diversify.

## DEALING WITH CLIENTS

Put yourself in the mind of your client. They want someone to supply a service, to see it done well and quickly, and have good results. They expect you to deliver. If they feel you don't, they will soon tell you.

They may not understand what you do or how, but if they respect your skills and the difference these can make to them, they could become an excellent client.

Do you have preconceptions about potential clients? Do you fear they may not be the sort of people you could get on with? Don't worry, there are lots of potential clients out there and you can carve out a specialism to work with who you'd like to, so long as you go about it the right way – by showing them they can't afford not to hire you!

Think about the customer service aspect of what you are doing. Shift your mindset from that of a hard-pressed writer or journalist up against a tight deadline to someone who is being paid to do a job directly by the person on the other end of the phone, or in an interminable meeting with you.

This can make a huge difference. Make all communication with them as professional as possible, thank them for their business and their help, be patient where needed and understand how busy they are, so you need to be as time-efficient as possible. Of course, you may be busy too, but when they are the client and they say 'jump', well, of course, your answer is 'how high?'

Brace yourself for negativity about your work – it happens and it doesn't matter how great a writer you are. Treat all such feedback professionally and tactfully.

Work together to help the client understand more about why your work, advice, knowledge or expertise should be valued. They may feel that you are 'just' a writer. But you are providing a precious commercial service that is as important as other business services, such as an accountant or solicitor.

Some would argue that they are even more important. Thanks to your writing skills, your clients have peace of mind that their communications are in a safe pair of hands and are giving the right impression.

## MANAGING CUSTOMER EXPECTATIONS

Make sure that they know what's happening. Keep them informed of progress, let them know when you have planned the work for and what the outcome will be. At the same time, explain politely and tactfully what's expected of them. Explain that you need them to come back to you about any changes needed in copy, in a certain time scale to do your job properly.

By aiming for clear, effective, professional communication at all times, you are marking yourself out as someone who means business and this will help build more of a rapport with someone working in a corporate environment and gain their respect.

## FINDING WORK

### Don't feel bad about walking away

Sometimes you will meet people who say they would love to use your services, but somehow it never happens. Perhaps you feel you just couldn't 'click' with them because there's something you distrust or sets alarm bells ringing from their manner or the way they talk to you. Perhaps they are trying to get lots of free advice from you. Go with your gut instinct and don't look back. You would be far more likely to end up regretting it if you did end up working for them.

### Be realistic about where your work will come from

There's something called the 80/20 rule, which says most of your work (up to 80 per cent) can come from just 20 per cent of your clients. You don't have to chase lots of customers, it can make sense to win more work from your existing ones. Luckily, it's easier to find new business from a current client than to put all the effort needed into finding new ones.

### Expect the unexpected

Some customers, despite spending money on your services, will insist they know better than you. They'll pick fault with everything you do and then they will string out paying. Get your money and run.

### Word of mouth works

My experience is that no amount of advertising can guarantee you any work in this area. But the 'word of mouth' that comes from doing a good job for someone who then recommends you, has been very beneficial.

With hand on heart, I can say we haven't gone down the (frankly terrifying) route of cold calling either. While ringing an editor with an idea or sending out a pitch could be viewed as 'cold calling' in journalism, the thought of doing this for copywriting work has no appeal, for a variety of reasons.

### Business networking can be worth it

You may be horrified or petrified by the prospect.

You may feel there could be nothing worse than a bunch of business people swapping small talk over coffee at a ridiculous hour in the morning, painting on a smile and doing your best to find work from the people in the room.

But there's plenty worse – having no work included.

Consider joining your local Chamber of Commerce and find out about other business networking groups. Try and go along, at least as a visitor, to see what they do and if you feel you could belong. Some are quite scary and could be excellent subject matter for a feature somewhere. But aside from that, you could promote your services as a copywriter. By attending as often as you can, you are 'farming' rather than 'hunting' – planting a seed that your services could one day be useful. Eight years on from joining my first group of this nature, my company continues to work for customers recommended to me within weeks of joining.

I did some free (alarm bells are ringing somewhere – please bear with me!) PR for a local business group and for a good while after, anyone who enquired of them about PR or copywriting was referred to me. If you are prepared to put in the groundwork, it will pay off.

Some of the business groups ask you to pay hundreds of pounds up front. There are several such groups in any town or city. One is BNI, Business Network International. An average seat at a BNI meeting is said to be worth £26,000 a year. You do have to commit to going every week if you can make it and you have to bring business for the other people round the table.

Network as much as you can bear. It will pay off so long as you hone your people skills, give off a warm and professional air and be interested in what other people are telling you. If you can spot opportunities for other members and pass them business, they'll want to do the same in return.

Making the most of networking:

- Find a group that meets at a time to suit you

- Where you feel comfortable with the people in it

- It's imperative you look beyond the members to understand who their clients and contacts are – these are the people whose work you are after

- Don't expect instant results

- Rehearse what you will say in any slot designed to give you the chance to highlight your writing business

- Be as specific as you can in letting people know what work you want and who for

### Strength in numbers – building 'strategic alliances'

Go and meet web designers and marketing people to offer out your services to their clients as a copywriter or proof reader. I've just completed a job to rewrite a brochure to a very tight deadline. Our customer is delighted and says he would like to use us again. The introduction came from the designer who was doing the brochure for them. She was someone who joined a women's networking group my colleague Carol set up, when she couldn't find one that met at a time to fit in with family commitments.

Forge working relationships with related individuals, companies or organisations. These could include:

- Graphic designers

- Web designers

- Social media agencies

- Marketing agencies

- PR agencies

- Freelance photographers

- Event organisers

### Marketing materials

Have business cards printed and make them look as professional as possible.

On your cards, don't just put name and contact details and basic job title – also list your services on the back. This sounds simple but is often overlooked. You could include:

- Journalism

- Copywriting

- Social media

Or expand as much as you like. Perhaps add photography to let people know you can sort this for them, collaborating with a trusted freelance colleague, or web design if you have struck up a viable working relationship.

## How to progress

Always trust your instincts and take everything any business adviser tells you with a pinch of salt.

Do not quote cheap because you are worried that customers will not want to pay more. You must value what you do and let them know that professional and well-written material is worth paying for.

As I said in Getting Started, if you win a customer on price, you will lose them on price. This is something I was warned about early on and boy did it come true.

Always be aware that business owners can have a very different approach and expectations, not to mention ways of communicating, than an editor.

At all times, remember they are the client so remain professional. If changes are made to your copy, discuss this calmly. If someone is paying you for your expertise, it can be frustrating to say the least, if they then want to change your work to something they prefer. You have to find the words to tell them firmly and respectfully why you have written something in a certain way. Put simply, it's based on your experience as a professional writer. If you don't feel you could manage to stay calm in such a situation, then this work is definitely not for you as it happens a lot.

## The nitty gritty

Always get an order form/contract signed up front. It's harsh but true that you cannot afford to do anything on trust. Some characters, unfortunately, will do anything to get out of paying. Establish stringent terms and conditions.

### Brace yourself: Cold calling

Make a wish list of the companies or not for profit organisations you'd like to be working for.

Set a time each week to research the companies on your list and add their details to a database (this can be a simple spreadsheet or word document) for future marketing.

Set yourself time each week to make a certain number of phone calls, send out flyers, letters or emails to potential new customers. Just like a pitch to an editor, effective follow up is essential to the success of any cold calling.

Compile a script of how you will introduce yourself and what you will say, practice saying it before you call.

Keep your database of clients, contacts, suppliers and business people you meet – set a goal to add at least 10 new contacts to the list every month.

### Maximising work through existing clients

Continue to market your services to clients you gain. If they take you on to write a brochure, once you have done a good job for them, perhaps ask if they need a blog.

Regularly speak to your clients about who they are working with and see if they will recommend you. Continue to market your services to your contacts, previous clients and people who've shown an interest in the past but didn't buy from you – because no means not yet. Also find out if people who supply you with services – your insurance broker, printer or solicitor even – could benefit from sound written material explaining what they do – they most probably would.

### Pricing and rates

Don't undervalue your services, experience or skill. If, through your contacts and writers' nose, you help place a client in a national newspaper, for example, make sure your fee reflects what a top notch job this is. An ad in a similar spot could set them back tens of thousands of pounds.

Understand how much your work in this area can help them. There are never any guarantees about what will happen once media material you have written appears in print or online, but two memorable instances for me remain. A client reporting gaining £36,000 of new business after a feature in a national newspaper and another telling me that they received an order worth £80,000 following an advertorial in our local evening newspaper.

## Top-down pricing

Start high and be prepared to negotiate. But don't quote so high you scare them off – doesn't sound too simple, I know. Perhaps dig around a little to find out how much your competitors are charging locally and add a little on top – because you're worth it and you are guaranteeing professional communication at all times, and anything else you can outline as a guarantee, to help your client understand why they would rather deal with you.

## How to set the rate for commercial writing jobs

Let's ponder the thorny issue of how to set a scale of charges for a commercial client.

They might ask you to write, sub, proof read, or edit their newsletters, other marketing material, website or press releases. They might ask you to do more stuff on top, like sending out the press releases, liaising with journalists, or getting their cuttings together.

So, are you going to charge per word, per page, per hour, or per project? Phew, that's quite a list, and I've seen various answers over the years. For most people, it comes down to a choice of per word or per hour. There are pros and cons to each approach:

### Per word pros:

You know where you stand.

If the work can be done quickly, it will be lucrative.

### Per word cons:

This doesn't take into account the time taken. What if you have to chase for amendments approval and wait for them to come back? What if they ask you to change wording you think is actually ok?

If it takes you an age to complete, through no fault of your own, then you can't do much about it. At least negotiate a rate for working on amendments if/when the client changes their mind.

### Per hour pros:

Billing for your time means you can more accurately forecast your earnings and know how much time you have left for other work.

If the work is additional marketing or administrative duties on top of the writing, then it makes sense.

### Per hour cons:

Clients might view this option with suspicion.

You might have to include an hourly breakdown to show what you have been spending your time doing.

If the work doesn't take long, then you might have been better charging per word.

What else do you need to take into consideration? When setting a rate, you really need to focus on what it costs you to work. What are your overheads and how much do you have to charge to cover them? Ask yourself if you are prepared to offer different rates in different circumstances, depending on whether this is an ongoing project or a one-off job.

Or look at the client's circumstances and decide can you, or should you, do them some sort of deal? Ultimately, that's your decision and nobody else's. But allow me to offer one tiny word of caution: don't get caught up in offering deals, discounts, or even freebies in the hope that someone will come back for more. They might not.

### When does the paid work begin?

As soon as you have agreed that it should. Don't drift from meeting to meeting, your time is money. Arrange for the paid work to start with a planning meeting and come up with a plan of what's needed as a result of the meeting. Try not to be tempted to do this before you have signed an order form. In some cases, it's sad but true that some people will take your ideas and run with them or employ someone else to put them into action. Keep your wits about you and don't dither in signing up a client who seems keen.

### Going over the time

When you confirm the work, include a contingency plan for what will happen if it takes much longer than expected. Do your best to stop this happening. Have a proposed fee arranged for extra time and make sure your client is aware of this.

### Client contracts

Have a process in place and be confident about it. Include what's chargeable time and what isn't, make sure you include planning and research time. Make sure your client is up to speed with your terms and conditions. Draw up your specific T&C and research what needs to go in. A solicitor may charge a one-off set fee to make sure all is as it should be and save you heartache in the long run. Ensure your customer is clear on your financial procedures and payment terms. Where you can, ask for some payment up front. Sort out on-going payment by standing order or BACS, for greater peace of mind.

## Nail the non-payers

Every business, big or small, can fall victim to cash flow problems, as mentioned already in chapter three. If your clients have signed all the necessary paperwork and don't pay on time, find out why. There may be a rare occasion where something has genuinely happened that has stalled payment – sadly, such as a bereavement or serious illness.

But when excuses continue, it's time to take action. Fifteen times was how many I gave it, chasing one particular invoice before launching court proceedings.

If they haven't paid after 30 days, as outlined in your terms and conditions, send a statement. Find out about interest on late payments.

You may also look into using a credit agency to access the money for you. These aren't baseball wielding heavies – even if some down on their luck freelancers may wish they were. Instead, they'll use letter, phone and email to track down the debtor on your behalf and seek a settlement, with a proportion going to them. It's tempting to think you don't want to let that proportion go, but when you tot up the stress and time needed in chasing these people, it can be worth it.

Sadly, some matters will end up in a small claims court. There have been three such occasions for my company. Two were in the first year and the last was a twisty tale of sleepless nights and deceit I wouldn't wish on anyone.

Don't forget – develop your sixth sense and walk away at the start, if needs be.

## Some useful paperwork

Adapt these templates for your own use, with relevant contact details and information about work planned or carried out.

# EXAMPLE QUOTE FOR PR SERVICES

CLIENT NAME
CLIENT ADDRESS
DATE
YOUR INITIALS / YOUR ORDER NO

Quote for media relations support

Dear

Thank you for your enquiry and for asking us to provide you with a quote for media relations support. I take pleasure in detailing below the work required and our costs.

Your needs:

To raise awareness of ...........................

To raise the profile of ..........................

We will:

- Interview authorised personnel

- Prepare a press release

- Advise on photography

- Seek authorisation

- Send material to named journalists

- Liaise with journalists as necessary

- Supply a contact report and updates on coverage wherever possible*

*Please note that we do not operate a cuttings service and are not able to monitor coverage in trade publications.

We recommend the use of good media photography to enhance the use of your press release and can obtain a quote for this if required.

Cost

Our terms

Work is invoiced at the end of (MONTH) or on completion with 30 days payment terms.

Clients are asked to sign a PR order form, including our terms and conditions, before work starts. Travel expenses to sites outside the immediate area are billed to the client after agreement.

This quote is valid for 30 days.

# EXAMPLE COVERING EMAIL FOR PRESS RELEASE APPROVAL

Dear (CLIENT'S NAME)

Thank you for taking the time to provide us with the information to write your press release. Please find attached a draft copy as agreed. Once you have approved it, we will send it to the following media:

If there are any other publications you would like us to target with this information, please let us know.

PLEASE NOTE: Any amendments you make to this draft should address factual inaccuracies only. The feature is written in the style of the media we are targeting, as a news or feature article, rather than an advertisement. Please trust our expertise in understanding the needs of those media so we can offer you the best chance of gaining coverage.

Our deadline for final copy to be sent to the media is _____ . We will not send anything to the media until the content has been agreed by all parties mentioned and/or quoted in the press release, so please advise us of your feedback and amendments before this date. Any delays may reduce the chances of use.

To inform us of any amendments, or to approve the draft, please contact us via telephone or return e-mail at the earliest opportunity.

Thank you again for your help and we look forward to receiving your feedback.

## EXAMPLE ORDER FORM

This document sets out specific information, as discussed between (CLIENT NAME) of (COMPANY NAME) (hereafter referred to as the client) and (YOUR NAME), regarding editorial work to commence on (MONTH/YEAR).

By signing this form, both parties agree to all information detailed in the order.

As discussed, (YOUR NAME) will provide editorial support to the client as follows:

We will:

- Interview authorised personnel

- Prepare a press release

- Seek authorisation

- Send material to named journalists

- Follow to publication

- Supply a contact report and updates on coverage wherever possible*

*Please note that we do not operate a cuttings service and are not able to monitor coverage in trade publications.

The client agrees to provide (YOUR NAME) with all necessary information to enable them to prepare media material and must make themselves available to PMR staff as and when necessary.

Approval will be sought from the client on all material before it is released to the media.

The agreed fee for this support is (YOUR FEE), to be invoiced at the end of (MONTH) or on completion with 30 days payment terms.

I have read and agree with the details of this order and also agree to abide by the terms and conditions overleaf.

If, once work has commenced, I decide to terminate the order, I understand that I will be required to pay 60% of the full amount, to cover work that will have already been undertaken by (YOUR NAME).

Client:

Signed:

Position:

Date:

Service provider: (YOUR NAME)

Signed:

Position:

Date:

Note: Make sure the client signs two copies of the order form, one for themselves and one for your records.

## EXAMPLE STANDING ORDER FORM

Payment by Standing Order

Please complete this form and forward it to your bank for processing as soon as possible.

Please pay: NAME ON YOUR BANK ACCOUNT, trading account number YOUR ACCOUNT NO at NAME OF YOUR BANK (sort code _____) the sum of £ _____ on 28th day of each month, to commence on and until you receive further notice from me/us in writing.

Your (THE CLIENT'S) business bank account details:

Bank name: ......................................................................................

Address: ...........................................................................................

Account Name: .................................................................................

Sort code: ............................... Account No: .................................

Reference: (your company name) ....................................................

Signature(s): ....................................................................................

Date: .................................................................................................

Banks will accept this as a formal agreement between you and a client. Once completed, this form must be sent to the client's bank to be processed. Alternatively, if the client uses online banking they can set up a standing order that way – you will need to provide them with the name of your bank account, account number and sort code.

# EXAMPLE GENTLE REMINDER LETTER

CLIENT NAME

CLIENT ADDRESS

DATE

Dear

Reference/ Account Number:

We note from our records that our invoice; _____ of £ _____ is as yet unpaid. This may be an oversight on your part or you may have a query on the invoice. Please can you let us know if this is the case, so that we can resolve this?

If you do not have a query on the account, we look forward to receiving your payment in the next few days.

If you have paid this account and this contact and your payment have crossed, then please accept our apologies.

# Doing Your
# Own PR

*If I fall asleep with a pen in my hand, don't remove it – I might be writing in my dreams.*

Danzae Pace

# Chapter 11
# Doing Your Own PR

## DON'T BE SHY

Nobody is going to be lining up to give you work in the early days of a freelance writing career. You need to prove yourself first. You'll need tenacity and determination by the bucketful. Are you an expert networker or does the thought of promoting yourself in person make your heart sink? The temptation is to think that you're a decent writer, so why bother?

Well, like it or not, getting out there and pressing the flesh can make or break a freelance career – so you'd better get over your reservations, fast.

If you think the world owes you a living as a freelance writer, then you are in the wrong job. You can't sit back and wait for the commissions to roll in.

You might have the most fantastic ideas in the world and can write like a dream but you also need to be able to convince people of this. You need to be able to chase customers, be they editors or commercial clients, and clinch that sale – all looking as tactful as possible, without annoying them and gaining a reputation for pestering.

Even when you have some work under your belt and have established a reputation as a safe pair of hands, don't forget just how much competition is out there – so you need to stay on top of your game.

There's no point in hiding your light under a bushel, you need to be broadcasting evidence of your skills and experience.

I've already outlined some benefits of networking – in real life and through social media – make these two potentially rather scary activities a priority, or at least give them a go. Remember, writers like Alex Gazzola said just 10 per cent of their time was spent writing? It's the other 90 per cent that matters when it comes to getting work. For Alex, his time will also be spent researching, planning and interviewing, but marketing is becoming increasingly important as your competition increases.

## FREELANCE LISTING SITES: ARE THEY WORTH IT?

They can be.

If you use the space well.

Don't just say you are a freelance writer who can deliver copy on time. That should be a given. Don't say you are 'professional' – that should also be taken for granted, too, or that you are friendly – I mean, that's very nice and everything but it won't make me commission you. Spell out your expertise and experience, list some of your commissions and explain what makes you different. We're back to banishing modesty again.

Joanne Mallon says: "Wouldn't it be lovely if you could just write your name on a flag, wipe it with a flake of gold, fly it in the air, then sit back and watch as a flurry of flakes of gold attached themselves to it like velcro?

"Sometimes I think this is the outcome people expect from listing sites that purport to bring in work for freelance journalists. Just pay a small fee, register your details, and the work will come flooding in. But do these sites actually work? Are people like you finding jobs through them?

"Well, yes and no. I talk to a lot of journalists, and the reports are mixed. For every person who's had work through listings sites, there are three or four who've had nothing at all. So it's a gamble, albeit with better odds than the lottery. Most recommendations have been for the NUJ listings –

maybe clients like hiring a writer with the 'official' stamp. Also getting yourself listed on a Gorkana alert gets the thumbs up."

Some of the main listings sites for freelance journalists are:

- NUJ Freelance Directory

- Journalism.co.uk

- Hold The Front Page

- Journalist Directory

- FreelanceUK

As a freelancer, you have to treat yourself as a business, and businesses invest in marketing. You may choose to invest in these sites and/or an all bells and whistles site of your own. Just don't make the mistake of not investing in any marketing at all. How can people buy from you if they don't know you exist?

## HOW TO HELP WORK FIND YOU

Joanne says:

LinkedIn seems to have been around for a donkey's age. With millions of users in the UK, even if you're not a member, you must have had a bucketful of those 'So and so wants to connect with you on LinkedIn' emails. I've had a semi-completed profile for a few years, but never paid much attention to it. But something has been changing, since I keep hearing about people getting writing work via LinkedIn, much as work for writers is beginning to be found via Twitter. So I decided to hop back on that donkey to see where it will take me.

The main tip I picked up when researching LinkedIn is that being at least a little active on the site, and having a complete profile, are the most important elements in helping recruiters find you. One of the things I had to do to complete my profile was to ask people who've worked with me for recommendations. It was pretty excruciating to do, but, surprisingly, once I'd asked, some really lovely testimonials came forth. So if you're wondering what I'm like to work with as a journalist, you can now find out.

One benefit of LinkedIn is that it ranks fairly highly on search engines, so if you haven't got a website yet, it's a good way to quickly and easily get yourself online. After all, nobody's likely to hire you if they can't find you.

The other thing I've done is take out a freelance listing at Journalism.co.uk. This costs £50 for a year, so, in theory, it should only take one commission to cover the cost, though, like any of these sites, it's a gamble from which you may not see any return. Here, my listing is much more pared down than LinkedIn, but I think it gets the essential information across. I'm not naive enough to think that simply registering with these sites will be enough to open the doors to an avalanche of work.

### REACTIVE MARKETING – APPLYING FOR A FREELANCE POSITION THAT'S ADVERTISED

CV tips from Joanne Mallon:

- Traditional careers advice doesn't really take account of the fact that CVs land on media recruiters' desks in their hundreds, and getting yours to stand out from the crowd takes work. The main points to remember are:

- Keep it brief – aim for one page, one and a half at most. In media land, the more experienced a person is, the shorter their CV becomes. Make every word earn its keep. I once saw a CV that included, under the 'Personal Details' section, the fascinating snippet 'I have two sisters, Sarah aged nine and Catherine aged 11'. You can probably leave out the name of the family dog as well.

- Work history goes before educational experience.

- Get someone to look at your CV and tell you what they notice in the first five seconds. This is about as long as an employer will look at it before deciding whether they want to read on. Make sure that what you want to be noticed actually sticks out.

Write a short covering letter (must be typed) saying who you are, what you want and why they should give it to you. The longer your letter, the less likely it is to be read. The same goes for your CV. No 17 year old needs a five page CV, though a surprising number of them have prepared one.

Personally, I don't think there's any need to put in your marital status – it seems a bit outmoded these days. Likewise, date of birth can be omitted, but only because it tends to make employers feel extra aged and haggard when they realise that people born after 1994 are now asking for work.

If you haven't got much relevant work experience, then list your education first – reverse this as you gain more work experience. Employers are much more interested in the work you've done than what you did for your dissertation. If you've got a degree then you don't need to list your GCSEs and A Levels individually.

You don't have to list your references on your CV, unless you want to highlight the fact that your referee is someone important. It's fine to put something along the lines of 'References available on request' as these will generally only be needed if you are under serious consideration for a job.

A prospective freelance employer may also ask someone else for a reference without your knowledge, particularly if they know someone who's worked for the same company as you. The more you work in it, the smaller you will find the media world to be, so be aware that it's not just the people you choose who may be asked to recommend you.

If you include a list of interests, don't include things that are basic staples of life, like reading, keep fit or the dreaded 'socialising'. You might as well put breathing and sleeping as well. Only include interests that are genuinely interesting and (preferably) relevant to the job.

## COVERING LETTER OR EMAIL

All your covering letter needs to be is a short note (typed, with impeccable grammar and spelling) saying who you are, what you want and why they should give it to you.

Always remember that the longer your letter, the less likely it is to be read. Just because it's called a covering letter doesn't mean it has to cover every aspect of your life and career to date – the potted highlights will do for now. The same goes for your CV. Editors and production companies are simply too busy to look at much more.

## PROACTIVE MARKETING – TELLING THE PEOPLE WHO MATTER ABOUT YOUR SKILLS

You need to market yourself to:

- Contacts who could become potential interviewees

- Contacts who could become customers

- Contacts who could provide valuable story generation ideas

- Editors who haven't heard of you yet

- Editors who you've already written for

- Potential commercial clients

- Existing commercial clients

Think of all the people you need to market yourself to and get on with it.

## NURTURE YOUR PEOPLE SKILLS

Don't hide behind your computer keyboard. Get out there, meet people, get yourself known in the right circles, attend the right events. Get in touch with contacts, potential clients and interviewees, even dreaded PR people. Go and have a coffee with them or maybe consider treating them to lunch, if you feel this could work. Of course, busy editors you haven't ever been in touch with before aren't going to jump at the chance to come and meet you, but once you have established a working relationship with them, there's no harm in suggesting you nip along for a coffee to discuss what they may be looking for in terms of ideas and future features. I've known writers who live a long way from the capital, arranging a day of meetings in London to do just that – lining up several appointments with contacts and editors in one day – and being delighted with the results.

## JOIN INFLUENTIAL GROUPS ACCORDING TO YOUR SPECIALISM

You may find the likes of the Guild of Health Writers, travel writers' groups and their local NUJ branch or media networking groups pretty useful. There may be the opportunity to meet guest speakers or respected senior figures in a chosen field. There's strength in numbers and these groups can help stop the isolation some freelancers report blights their day-to-day work.

## GET WEBWISE

Set up a website to showcase your work. This needn't be expensive. There are several free systems that allow you to present a homepage and a portfolio. Have a look at other writers' sites, see which they have used and what you like. Ask around on forums or through networking – find recommendations for hosting and/or design you can trust.

Include case studies of work you have done for a range of clients or that underline a specialism. If you are so minded, include references or testimonials from current or former clients – some people don't like asking or find this a bit cheesy.

Perhaps a link to the testimonials on your LinkedIn page could work well if you share their view – it's accepted practise to illustrate these on the professional network.

Make sure your contact details are prominent. Never assume setting up a website in itself is enough to sell your work. Work hard to promote it – on business cards, in your email signature, and not forgetting telling people in real life.

Point editors to your site, or a relevant section when you pitch ideas to them. Keep it updated with latest published pieces or choose a select few to illustrate what you are capable of.

Consider linking to other freelancers or interesting and relevant news sites or professional associations. Here's hoping they'll consider doing the same in return.

## SEARCH ENGINE OPTIMISATION

Use free resources to find out as much as you can about how to help potential customers find you on the web – think of what search terms they will use when looking for you and use those in your text on your website. You may consider it unlikely that an editor will be browsing the web looking for new writers, but it does happen. Potential commercial clients are far more likely to be looking, though, so think about what you need to include about your copywriting services to make it as easy as possible to get work from them.

## DEVELOP YOUR OWN BRAND – AND SHOUT ABOUT IT

You may hate the thought of being considered a brand. I know I did. But, like it or not, that's increasingly how clients will think of you.

Present your expertise in your chosen field, plugging your background as well as your writing skills. If you used to be an accountant, teacher, fireman or nurse, tell editors this and make sure you pounce when opportunities for you to call on your previous experience crop up.

## WHAT GOES AROUND, COMES AROUND

This is a key principle behind networking – you scratch my back and I'll scratch yours. In recent years, I've been contacted by national newspapers and radio stations looking for interviewees thanks to my blog. I've been recommended for jobs by contacts made on an online forum and directly offered work by editors via Twitter.

For Joanne Mallon, networking is obligatory – and not just about standing round drinking warm wine and making small talk.

She says: "It doesn't matter how good you are if an editor won't open your emails or take your calls. For those of us still developing our careers, networking can work wonders – the more people that know, trust or like you, the better.

"People dismiss others as 'shameless networkers', as if it's something to feel ashamed of, but it's about building relationships.

"You should talk to people all the time and, more importantly, listen to what they have to say. Don't just keep in touch when you're after a story, be genuinely interested in what they're doing all the time. You never know where a conversation may lead.

"If you write for an editor but have never met them, make a point of inviting them for coffee or dropping by to see them. If you live outside London, you might have to take a day out to do this, but it's worth it. You learn things in face-to-face meetings that you can't pick up any other way."

As we saw in chapter eight, social networking websites are opening up more opportunities and you can use your own blog to forge contacts, putting you in front of people who didn't previously know you existed.

You also have to beware of what can happen if you don't network. An interviewee once told me he'd looked for me on LinkedIn – and hadn't found me there. His conclusion was to wonder if I really existed.

### YOUR NAME OR COMPANY NAME?

My company is called Passionate Media. These days I joke that it seemed a good idea at the time. It has raised eyebrows and it has made people laugh. I'll let you imagine whether I consider this a good or bad thing. Actually, it varies from day to day.

I used a company name because I thought it sounded more professional and I chose Passionate Media because I considered it sent out the right message. I would promote the fact for commercial clients that I felt I was:

- Passionate about people

- Passionate about business

- Passionate about getting it right

The sound of this may make you cringe and I understand that. But these three little points helped me get an awfully large amount of work, so I swallowed my pride and got on with it. People told me I shouldn't be so modest and that these slogans set me apart from the competition. Think about what straplines or slogans you could attach to your services. These days, where you see the words Passionate Media in letter headings or on business cards and so on, you will see a much more muted: "Inspirational Communications" – I prefer that by far.

For me, Linda Jones Associates or Linda Jones Writing Services was never going to be an option – there are just too many of us about. Think seriously about what course of action you would like to take and do what's right for you.

In the early days, I encountered clients who said they couldn't work with me if I was seen too much as an individual as opposed to a commercial enterprise, so that swung it for me.

## GET IT RIGHT

If you want to find a business name, here are some tips to help:

- Relate your choice of name to your own circumstances – is there a quirky or memorable name connected to your life that you could use?

- Don't call your company something beginning with z – that will put you at the bottom of too many lists

- Make sure your company name is easy to remember, not too long and easy to say

- Consider alliteration to make your name more memorable

- Don't spend any money on designers for company literature until you are 100 per cent sure of what you want – a mistake I would have liked to avoid

- Avoid fashionable names – they will date too quickly

- For kudos, you need something that suggests professionalism, class and expertise

## MARKETING YOURSELF TO EDITORS

Yes, sending a pitch they can't turn down and continuing to do so is the most fail-safe way of winning work from an editor. But think how much more likely they are to commission you again if you have been able to keep in touch and help since, or you have met them at a networking do, shown how you can drive traffic to their site by promoting your articles through social media or have been out to lunch with them. It does happen and it can work. Touches like always saying thank you for the work or sending a Christmas card may seem, depending on your point of view, like stating the obvious, or totally uncalled for. I hope you can see that being nice to editors can help stand you in good stead and that you should develop appropriate customer relations skills.

## THERE'S A FINE LINE

Don't be a nuisance. Editors are busy people, don't publicly tweet them or leave messages on a facebook page asking if they got your email. How quickly can they realistically be expected to come back to you? They may not have asked you to get in touch, after all.

## DON'T FORGET ABOUT JOB ADS

Okay, so these are mainly for staff jobs. But tucked away in the same ad may also be a call out for freelance contributors. Even if there isn't such an appeal, you have nothing to lose with a polite and succinct inquiry as to whether there are any opportunities.

## EDITORS TALK TO EACH OTHER

There's no better advert than word of mouth. Deliver what you say you will or you could find yourself in trouble. If you can't work on a commission because of a holiday or illness, consider passing it on to someone else. You may bristle at this thought and at the prospect of work being lost, but you gain the chance of someone doing the same for you.

## JOIN FORCES FOR MORE PITCHING POWER

Check out the sections about building strategic alliances in chapter 10. These can also work well for some writers when they approach different potentially paying markets – working together with a photographer, for example. Or, of course, as publications tighten their belts, they may favour someone who can supply words and pictures themselves. I can't and prefer to work with someone. I can find them work and they can do the same for me.

## CONTACT NOT FOR PROFIT, LOCAL AUTHORITY AND CHARITABLE ORGANISATIONS

Find out what writing they have to do – usually a mountain of it – and offer your services, once you've established there's a budget of course. Personally, I have found that this is an area where volunteering can pay off – so long as you go into it with your eyes open and make the most of other (paid) opportunities this may bring you. I volunteered for a charity for more than a year before talking myself into the job of magazine editor with them (I did want to volunteer anyway – it wasn't for the job!).

## MARKET YOURSELF TO PEOPLE YOU CAN WRITE ABOUT

Consider starting your own email newsletter, so long as you feel confident that you have enough to say. In each edition, remind them of all your services, link to published work and/or offer advice.

## KEEP IN TOUCH

Just let people know you are still around. Phone now and again to see if they have anything that could spark a feature for you.

## FEATURE POSTCARDS

These have worked well. We printed postcards appealing for people with 'human interest' stories to get in touch. The wording set out what sort of stories we were looking for and advised how to get in touch.

## GET TO KNOW PR PEOPLE – BUT DON'T RELY ON THEM

These days there are far more people whose job it is to control a media image for a client than there ever was. You need to be on relevant contact lists for PRs working in areas you are interested in, to keep up with developments. But keep your wits about you – it's not your job to regurgitate press releases – no editor is going to pay for that. Arguably, this may happen more in cash-strapped news rooms but you should avoid it like the plague. You shouldn't be suggesting submitting anything to an editor that could be done in-house.

## A POSITIVE EXAMPLE

Respected health writer and editor Rachel Newcombe says:

"In the early stages, definitely having a website and making sure the SEO was good for me in terms of my own PR, so it came up in the top 10 results for certain key phrases (on one phrase at least, it came up as the first result).

"I've also found paid listings in various online journalism/writing directories extremely good. In later years, networking through Twitter has been great and also blogging."

## USEFUL ADDRESSES

HM Revenue & Customs
**www.hmrc.gov.uk**
Companies House:
Tel : 0870 33 33 636 or 02920 381245
Email: **enquiries@companies-house.gov.uk**
**www.companieshouse.gov.uk**

Main office :
Companies House
Crown Way
Maindy
Cardiff CF14 3UZ

HM Treasury
The Correspondence & Enquiry Unit
2/W1 HM Treasury
1 Horse Guards Road
LONDON SW1A 2HQ
Tel : 020 7270 4558
Fax : 020 7270 4861
**www.hm-treasury.gov.uk**

Chambers of Commerce
The British Chambers of Commerce
65 Petty France
London SW1H 9EU
Tel: 020 7654 5800
Fax: 020 7654 5819
Email: **info@britishchambers.org.uk**
**www.britishchambers.org.uk**
For business services enquiries contact:
The British Chambers of Commerce
Greyfriars Court, 14 Queen Victoria Road

Coventry CV1 3PJ
Tel: 024 7669 4484
Fax: 024 7669 5844

BNI
Business Network International Ltd
BNI House
Church Street
Rickmansworth WD3 1BS
Office: 01923 891 999
Fax: 01923 891 998
Email: **bniuk@eurobni.com**
**www.bni.eu/uk**

WINGS
Women's Independent Networking Groups (Midlands)
**www.wings.uk.net**

NCTJ Training Ltd
The New Granary
Station Road
Newport, Saffron Walden
Essex CB11 3PL
Tel : 01799 544014
Fax: 01799 544015
Email: **info@nctj.com**
**www.nctj.com**

The Journalism Diversity Fund
NCTJ
The New Granary
Station Road
Newport, Saffron Walden
Essex CB11 3PL
Tel : 01799 544014

Fax: 01799 544015
Email: journalismdiversityfund@nctj.com
www.journalismdiversityfund.com

NUJ – National Union of Journalists
Headland House
308-312 Gray's Inn Road
LONDON WC1X 8DP
Tel: 020 7843 3705
Fax: 020 7837 8143
Email: info@nuj.org.uk
www.nuj.org.uk

Chartered Institute of Public Relations
CIPR Public Relations Centre
52-53 Russell Square
LONDON WC1B 4HP
Tel : 020 7631 6900
Fax: 020 7631 6944
Email: info@cipr.co.uk
www.cipr.co.uk

The Chartered Institute of Journalists
2 Dock Offices
Surrey Quays Road
LONDON SE16 2XU
Tel: 020 7252 1187
Fax: 020 7232 2302
Email: memberservices@cioj.co.uk
www.cioj.co.uk

Society for Proofreaders and Editors
Apsley House
176 Upper Richmond Road, Putney
LONDON SW15 2SH

Tel: 020 8785 6155
Email: **administrator@sfep.org.uk**
**www.sfep.org.uk**

Society of Editors
University Centre
Granta Place
Mill Lane
Cambridge CB2 1RU
Tel : 01223 304080
Fax: 01223 304090
Email: **office@societyofeditors.org**
**www.societyofeditors.co.uk**

The Authors' Licensing and Collecting Society
ALCS Ltd
The Writers' House
13 Haydon Street
LONDON EC3N 1DB
Tel : 020 7264 5700
Fax: 020 7264 5755
Email: **alcs@alcs.co.uk**
**www.alcs.co.uk**

## FURTHER READING

Press Gazette
**www.pressgazette.co.uk**

Writers' News & Writing Magazine
**www.writers-online.co.uk**

The New Writer
**www.thenewwriter.com**

Online journalism blog
**www.onlinejournalismblog.com**

Journalism.co.uk
www.journalism.co.uk

JournoBiz forums
www.journobiz.com/forums

Freelance Advisor
www.freelanceadvisor.co.uk/

NUJ Rate for the job guide
http://www.londonfreelance.org/rates/

Better Payment Practice Campaign and late payment interest calculator
http://payontime.co.uk/

Mistakes writers make blog
http://mistakeswritersmake.blogspot.co.uk

Bubblecow blog
http://bubblecow.co.uk/blog/

Womag writer's blog
http://womagwriter.blogspot.co.uk/

My Writing Blog by Nick Daws
www.mywritingblog.com

Authonomy
www.authonomy.com

Apostrophe Protection Society
http://www.apostrophe.org.uk/

Freelance Writing Tips launched by Craig McGinty and Linda Jones
www.freelancewritingtips.com

My Writers Circle
www.mywriterscircle.com

# RECOMMENDED READING

Wanna be a writer? by Katie Fforde and Jane Wenham-Jones

The Renegade Writer: A Totally Unconventional Guide to Freelance Writing Success by Linda Formichelli & Diana Burrell

The Writers' ABC Checklist by Lorraine Mace and Maureen Vincent-Northam

The Online Journalism Handbook: Skills to Survive and Thrive in the Digital Age by Paul Bradshaw and Lisa Rohumaa Longman (June 2011)

Start your own home based business by Nick Daws

Writing for journalists by Wynford Hicks, Sally Adams and Harriet Gilbert

The Freelance Writer's Handbook: How to make money and enjoy your life by Andrew Crofts (Piatkus Books)

Eat, Shoots and Leaves, The Zero Tolerance Guide to Punctuation by Lynne Truss

Essential English: For Journalists, Editors and Writers by Harold Evans

The Well-Fed Writer: Financial Self-Sufficiency as a Freelance Writer in Six Months or Less by Peter Bowerman

From Pitch to Publication; Everything You Need to Know to Get our Novel Published by Carole Blake

The Novelist's Guide: Powerful Techniques for Creating Character, Dialogue and Plot by Margaret Geraghty

Writers' and Artists' Yearbook

The Writer's Handbook by Barry Turner

On Writing by Stephen King

McNae's Essential Law for Journalists by Tom Welsh, Walter Greenwood and David Banks

# Index